P9-CBV-721

John,

Enjoy finding your son's name.

We hope you get as much joy from your little boy as we did,

love -

Mom + Pops

Boy Baby Names for 2017

Hannah Crawford

ISBN:153756742X

ISBN-13: 978-1537567-426

Penguinies@outlook.com

DEDICATED

This book is dedicated to my two gorgeous little boys Troy and Jemai. I would also like to dedicate this book to Bradley for blessing me with my second son. I love you all with the whole of my heart, always & forever.

Boy Baby Names for 2017

Introduction

The Boy Baby Names for 2017 Book has over 1700 first names to help you to decide on the right name for your baby. There is a wide variety to choose from with both modern and classic names listed alphabetically. With pronunciations, origins and meanings all included to give you a better understanding of each name.

The Boy Baby Names for 2017 Book can help you to pick a suitable baby name that suits your child and family surname. Each name has been divided up into easily readable sections. Agreeing on a special baby name can be one of the most difficult yet rewarding decisions that any parent can make during their lifetime. This book can help make choosing a baby name easy and lots of fun.

Contents

Boy Baby Names for 2017

How to choose a baby name

Finding out that you are expecting a baby is one of the most joyous and happiest moments that you can experience in your life. Some parents already have name choices and know what they want to call their baby long before they find out that they are pregnant, however, for others, this can be a daunting and difficult task.

I know when I was expecting my first son I found it extremely difficult to pick a name that I thought would be perfect for him, and a couple of months before he was born, I finally settled on a name. However, once my son was born and I held him in my arms for the first time, I quickly realised the name that I had spent so many months deciding on didn't seem to suit him and I was back to square one.

Names are a part of everyday life and culture; they can have a great significance to the child who receives the name and also to the societies that give them. A baby name is not only a name that will be with your infant throughout its childhood; it is a name that will stick with them for life. To add to the pressure, there is such a huge range and variety of baby names to choose from and to consider that the task can seem tremendously overwhelming. The *Boy Baby Names for 2017* Book of Baby Names has suggested a few helpful tips when it comes to choosing a baby name that is right for you, your child and family.

Where to start

Decide what are the most important factors for you and your partner when choosing a baby name; this may include any family traditions, uniqueness, popularity, celebrity influences, or gender.

It is a good idea to make a list of your favourite baby names and share them with your partner who can do the same with you. Combine your favourite names into one list and use this as a starting point. If you do not have a partner, you could make a list with a good friend or a family member and have lots of fun listening to each other's name suggestions. You can add more names along the way; no doubt you will have lots of name suggestions from family members, friends and even from strangers that you can also add to your list of possible baby names.

One popular choice for parents-to-be is to name their newborn baby after a grandparent, relative or an ancestor. Your baby's heritage will always be an essential aspect of who they are as an individual. Choosing a name that is important to you or your family can reflect this. Some families have a strict naming tradition that dates back generations. Although you should never let anybody pressure you into naming your baby something that you are not keen on or do not really like. Instead, you could consider using them as middle names to honour your family traditions. This can make the process a whole lot simpler. However, this choice is not for everybody, for me personally this was not an option.

Unique names

For some parents one of the most important aspects when deciding on a name for their baby is the uniqueness of it. The obvious advantage in choosing a unique or unusual baby name is how it can stand out from the crowd and be remembered throughout time. Some people like the shock factor that a unique name can generate

for the child. The downside of picking a unique or unusual name is pronunciation; numerous people may struggle to pronounce your child's name which could bring negative attention to your child for all of the wrong reasons. The name may be hard for others to spell and constantly having to correct people who cannot spell or pronounce the name can become tiring, especially for your child when he/she is at school.

Choosing a unique baby name can allow the parents to use and to also show off their own personal creativity. This could be a lot of fun, albeit if you choose this option, you should prepare yourself for being asked numerous questions about your chosen baby name and the reasons behind it. Modern celebrities often pick unusual and unique names for their babies which can generate a lot of publicity for them and their new-born child. Another thing to consider if you are looking for a unique baby name is that the name may sound cute and adorable when the baby is young, although when the child grows up into an adult, the name could possibly sound outrageous and somewhat ridiculous. Some parents might feel too embarrassed to consider using a unique baby name for their child and may prefer to opt for a more traditional name instead.

A rising trend with parents who are opting to pick unique baby names for their children is for them to use names that begin with or have the letter 'x' in them. The reason being that the names are thought to have a unique and edgy style and sound over other baby names. Angelina Jolie facilitated this popularisation by choosing names that had the letter 'x' in them for three of her five children, Pax, Maddox, and Knox.

Boys Names with the letter X	Girls Names with the letter X
1. Alexander	1. Alexa
2. Axel	2. Alexandra
3. Baxter	3. Alexis
4. Braxton	4. Beatrix
5. Bronx	5. Dixie
6. Dixon	6. Exene
7. Felix	7. Jaxine
8. Huxley	8. Moxie
9. Jax	9. Oxsana
10. Lennox	10. Phoenix
11. Madox	11. Roxanne
12. Maxim	12. Trixie
13. Maxwell	13. Xena
14. Pax	14. Xenia
15. Rex	15. Xiomara

Name meanings and connotations

Name meanings can be an important attribute to a family when considering a baby name. Some names have different meanings in different cultures and countries that have evolved from different languages, this can be a little confusing when deciding on a baby name. However, it can also be a positive as the meaning of the name may be more desirable in one culture than it is in another.

Some names may have personal connotations, even though your partner may love one name it might remind you of somebody that you don't get along with, or it could be the same name as an ex-partner or ex-friend, etc. You may have found a perfect name that you have always loved and wanted to give to your newborn baby however a friend or family member may have got there first and used the same name for their child. This might put you off from using the name for your own baby. Alternatively, you may love the name so much that you might decide to give the name to your baby anyway.

Pronunciation and sound

How to pronounce your baby's name and how it sounds when spoken aloud is often an essential element to all parents when choosing a name for their baby. A name could sound harmonious and pleasant, alternatively, it may sound harsh or brash which could be an ultimate decision maker. The name could also be extremely difficult for others to pronounce which could end up completely changing your opinion on the name.

Surnames

Considering your child's surname is a common practice for a lot of parents when choosing a baby name as it can help you to pick the right name. Some parents prefer to avoid names that rhyme with their surnames while others favour this option. Names that flow with your baby's last surname can help you to narrow your list down. People can be ever so cruel when it comes to nicknames which are usually given to a person during their adolescent years. This is something that you could consider when choosing a name for your baby, especially when it comes to the initials. Check what the initials spell out, for example, Georgina Imogen Thomas sounds like a nice name. However, the initials are somewhat unfortunate in what they spell out. This is something that could be picked up on by classmates, family members, work colleagues and even by strangers. This could be rather embarrassing and unpleasant for your child to have to experience throughout their life.

Can you agree on a name?

One of the reasons why choosing a baby name can become so difficult for a lot of parents is because it's a decision that both you and your partner often make together. Finding a name that two people like can be tricky and take a lot longer than if it was just one person who was making the decision on their own. However, if your partner strongly disagrees with one of your favourite choice names you should listen to their opinions and not force a name that isn't liked or appreciated by both sides as it can cause conflict and resentment. If you both make a list of favourite baby names you can look through each other's lists and then discuss the pros and cons of each one, this could help the process dramatically. Your partner may have some really

great ideas for names that you hadn't thought about before. Therefore, it's always good to share your honest thoughts and opinions with one and other.

Does the name suit your baby?

As I mentioned previously, I spent months looking through and researching baby names until I found one that I thought would be perfect for my son just before he was born. When I finally decided on a name that I thought would be ideal for my child I was a hundred percent sure that this was going to be his name for life. However, as soon as my son arrived into this world I quickly realised that the name that I was so certain about before did not suit him or his little personality at all. We spent the next few days thinking up alternative names until we found the perfect one that did suit him to the T. Luckily you are given 42 days after your baby is born to register the name officially in England, Wales and Northern Ireland. This means you could try out alternative names and see which one best suits him/her before you make your final decision.

Name popularity

Names that are already extremely popular and are in the top ten can be a decision maker when deciding on a baby name. Some parents like to pick a popular baby name, while others prefer to choose a name that is out of the top ten or even the top hundred baby names category. Celebrities can also have a drastic effect on the popularisation of a baby name. The name Harper has seen the largest rise in girls' names; this is most likely due to the celebrity couple Victoria and David Beckham who chose the name for their daughter in 2011. The name Eric rose by 314% in 2014 after celebrity Simon Cowell chose it for his first born son.

The media can also have a huge influence in popularising baby names in addition to celebrities. The popular television series, Game of Thrones has recently inspired some parents with their choice of baby names particularly, those who gave birth to baby girls. Almost two hundred and fifty babies have been named Arya, and fifty-three babies have been named Khaleesi. Although the male names have proven to be less influential, they have still been rather popular with eighteen babies being called Theon and seventeen babies named Tyrion.

Likewise, the release of a new Disney movie always tends to influence people's choices in baby names. Recently there has been a dramatic rise in babies being named Elsa, which was the name used for the Ice Queen in the animated blockbuster 2013 film Frozen.

Popular Baby Names in Regions within England

Region	Girls	Boys
East	Olivia	Oliver
East Midlands	Olivia	Oliver
West Midlands	Amelia	Muhammad
North East	Amelia	Oliver
North West	Amelia	Oliver
Yorkshire & The Humber	Amelia	Oliver
London	Amelia	Muhammad
South East	Amelia	Oliver
South West	Amelia	Oliver

The Top Baby Names in England

Girls	Boys
1. Amelia	1. Oliver
2. Olivia	2. Jack
3. Emily	3. Harry
4. Isla	4. George
5. Ava	5. Jacob
6. Ella	6. Charlie
7. Jessica	7. Noah
8. Isabella	8. William
9. Mia	9. Thomas
10. Poppy	10. Oscar

The Top Baby Names in Wales

Girls	Boys
1. Amelia	1. Oliver
2. Olivia	2. Jacob
3. Ava	3. Charlie
4. Isla	4. Jack
5. Emily	5. Noah
6. Ella	6. Alfie
7. Mia	7. Oscar
8. Isabella	8. William
9. Lilly	9. George
10. Evie	10. Harry

The Top Baby Names in Scotland

Girls	Boys
1. Emily	1. Jack
2. Sophie	2. Oliver
3. Olivia	3. James
4. Isla	4. Lewis
5. Ava	5. Alexander
6. Jessica	6. Charlie
7. Amelia	7. Logan
8. Ella	8. Lucas
9. Lucy	9. Harris
10. Lily	10. Daniel

The Top Baby Names in Northern Ireland

Girls	Boys
1. Emily	1. James
2. Ella	2. Jack
3. Grace	3. Noah
4. Sophie	4. Charlie
5. Olivia	5. Daniel
6. Anna	6. Oliver
7. Amelia	7. Matthew
8. Aoife	8. Harry
9. Lucy	9. Tomas
10. Ava	10. Jake

The Top Baby Names in France

Girls	Boys
1. Manon	1. Armand
2. Jade	2. Jules
3. Louise	3. Lucas
4. Alice	4. Léo
5. Camille	5. Gabriel
6. Chloé	6. Arthur
7. Lēa	7. Louis
8. Lou	8. Hugo
9. Emma	9. Tom
10. Charlotte	10. Sacha

The Top Baby names in Spain

Girls	Boys
1. Lucía	1. Hugo
2. María	2. Daniel
3. Paula	3. Pablo
4. Daniela	4. Alejandro
5. Martina	5. Álvaro
6. Carla	6. Adrián
7. Sara	7. David
8. Sofía	8. Mario
9. Valeria	9. Diego
10. Julia	10. Javier

The top baby names in America

Girls	Boys
1. Emma	1. Noah
2. Olivia	2. Liam
3. Sophia	3. Mason
4. Ava	4. Jacob
5. Isabella	5. William
6. Mia	6. Ethan
7. Abigail	7. James
8. Emily	8. Alexander
9. Charlotte	9. Michael
10. Harper	10. Benjamin

The Top Baby Names in Australia

Girls	Boys
1. Olivia	1. Oliver
2. Ava	2. Jack
3. Charlotte	3. James
4. Mia	4. Noah
5. Isla	5. William
6. Sophie	6. Thomas
7. Grace	7. Ethan
8. Amelia	8. Mason
9. Ruby	9. Liam
10. Chloe	10. Lachlan

The *Boy Baby Names for 2017* Book of Baby Names predicts another year of vintage baby names hitting the top spots. Our top ten predictions are;

Top Ten Baby Name Predictions for 2017	
1. Amelia	1. George
2. Ava	2. Oliver
3. Olivia	3. Jack
4. Isabella	4. William
5. Isla	5. Harry
6. Emily	6. Noah
7. Mia	7. Charlie
8. Jessica	8. Oscar
9. Isabella	9. Lewis
10. Poppy	10. Thomas

Celebrities

New baby name trends often emerge once a popular celebrity has a baby. Both celebrities and pop culture can impact and generate a sudden usage of a baby name, creating a remarkable rise in popularity within such a short period of time. Prominence is often given to a name after a celebrity has chosen it for their own child.

Celebrity culture can have a huge impact on people, influencing parents and helping to inspire them with baby names. Some celebrities like to choose traditional and more vintage baby names for their child, while other celebrities like to turn their backs on tradition and prefer to pick a unique name that can seem outrageous to some. Celebrities can feel pressurised and incentivised to create a unique baby name for their child, the use of objects such as Apple and Pilot are becoming frequently used for baby names along with the use of verbs.

Either way, celebrities can influence parents across the globe on their choice of baby names. The more popular a celebrity, the more influence they are likely to have on the public.

Some of the most talked about celebrity baby names are;

Kim Kardashian and Kanye West

One of the most famous and recent controversial baby names came from the reality TV star Kim Kardashian, and her rapper husband, Kanye West. The celebrity couple named their daughter North West in 2013. The name is said to have been chosen as it represents the highest power. The couple had their second child in December 2015, Saint West.

Lil' Kim and Papers

Lil' Kim and Papers welcomed their baby girl into the world back in June 2014. They named their daughter Royal Reign, which didn't seem so much of a surprise as rapper Lil' Kim likes referring to herself as the 'Queen Bee.'

Liv Tyler and David Gardner

Liv Tyler and her boyfriend choose a nautical baby name for the son Sailor Gene Gardner in early 2015.

Tom Fletcher and Giovanna Fletcher

McBusted star Tom Fletcher and his author wife Giovanna Fletcher named their son Buzz Michelangelo. The married couple insist that the name was not inspired by the famous Toy Story character, Buzz Lightyear. Tom and Giovanna welcomed their second son into the world, Buddy Bob Fletcher in February 2016.

Megan Fox and Brian Austin Green

Hollywood stars Megan Fox and Brian Austin Green raised eyebrows after they named their second son Bodhi Ransom in early 2014. The Buddhism-inspired name Bodhi means awakened or enlightenment on the path to Nirvana. Megan and Brian are expecting their third child in 2016. There has already been much speculation about the possible baby name.

Omarion and Apryl Jones

The R&B singer Omarion and his partner Apryl Jones named their son Megaa Omari Grandberry in 2014. The name is definitely distinctive and one of a kind.

Ciara and Future

Singers Ciara and Future named their son Future Zahir in 2014. Naming your child after its father has been a popular tradition for centuries. However, the name Future was actually taken from his father's stage name.

Holly Madison

Former Playboy model, Holly Madison received quite a lot of criticism after she named her daughter Rainbow Aurora in 2013. Holly defended her baby name choice by claiming that she had always loved the name Rainbow because it is such a pretty and unusual name. She also revealed that the name was inspired by somebody that she went to school with who also had the same name Rainbow. Holly and her husband are currently expecting baby number two due in 2016.

Alicia Silverstone

Hollywood actress Alicia Silverstone named her son Bear Blu back in May 2011. The name is unique and Silverstone claims that most people find the name to be "Super cute."

Nicole Ritchie and Joel Madden

Reality TV star Nicole Ritchie and her musician husband Joel Madden named their son Sparrow James Midnight. Nicole explained that she really liked the name Sparrow which was influenced by Captain Jack Sparrow from The Pirates of the Caribbean. Madden is said to like the name for different reasons. Nicole also revealed that she liked how the name sounded with her daughter's name, Harlow.

Gwen Stefani and Gavin Rossdale

Although musicians Gwen Stefani and Gavin Rossdale have never disclosed the origins of their son's name, Zuma Nesta Rock. There has been much speculation and theories surrounding their baby name choice. Many people believe that Zuma is named after a beach in Malibu where Rossdale is said to have had an epiphany. Nesta is believed to have come from Gwen Stefani's love of reggae music, as it is also the given name of Bob Marley. Finally, Rock is thought to be inspired by the genre of music.

Nicholas Cage

Possibly due to his love of comics, Hollywood actor Nicholas Cage notoriously named his son after the Krypton name of Superman, Kal-El.

Penn Jillette

Renowned magician Penn Jillette believes that it is cruel for parents to give a child a name that others already have, therefore he and his wife decided to call their daughter a very unique and rememberable name, Moxie Crimefighter.

Pop culture names

Movies and successful television shows have had a huge influence on baby names, along with books and music for decades. Names that are given to the leading protagonists typically see an instant increase in the popularity of baby names. The Twilight Saga has popularised the names, Isabella and Jacob, along with other hugely successful names that have been given to vampires in films and television shows such as True Blood and the Vampire Diaries.

Reality television can also have an immense influence on the choice of baby names. Since the Kardashians shot to fame in 2007, there has been a huge rise in baby names beginning with the letter 'K'. The globally successful US television series, Teen Mom has sparked a spectacular surge in the popularity of the baby names Maci and Bentley. Maci Bookout is one of the show's original cast members, and Bentley is the name of her eldest son.

Disney movies inspire people every day with their fairytale stories and beautiful characters. The unique personalities and the inner qualities that the leading characters boast, quite often influence parents-to-be with a list of baby names. In 2010,

the girls name Tiana more than doubled with parents giving this name to their daughters after Disney released The Princess and The Frog. Disney princesses have had a huge impact on baby names over the years.

However, it is not only the Disney princesses that inspire parents with new baby names, Disney films have featured a succession of unforgettable heroines and heroes which parents are naming their children after.

Disney Princess Names	
Anna	Frozen
Ariel	The Little Mermaid
Aurora	Sleeping Beauty
Belle	Beauty and The Beast
Elsa	Frozen
Jasmine	Aladdin
Merida	Brave
Moana	Moana
Mulan	Mulan
Pocahontas	Pocahontas
Tiana	The Princess and the Frog
Tinkerbell	Peter Pan

Disney Male Names	
Buzz	Toy Story
Eric	The Little Mermaid
Finn	Cars
Gaston	Beauty and the Beast
Milo	Atlantis
Peter	Peter Pan
Hans	Frozen
Kristoff	Frozen
Remy	Ratatouille
Rex	Toy Story
Sebastian	The Little Mermaid
Woody	Toy Story

Paying homage to a historical figure, classic movie star, musician or celebrity by naming your child after them is a way of demonstrating the admiration and respect that you have for that individual. Hollywood actor Vin Diesel is the latest celebrity to pay homage to a fellow actor by naming his daughter Pauline after the death of his co-star Paul Walker, who tragically died in a car wreck in 2013. Mariah Carey named her daughter Monroe after one of her favourite idols and film stars Marilyn Monroe. Liam Gallagher named his son Lennon after his favourite Beatles star John Lennon.

Different Spellings

Creating new or using different spellings can make your babies name less traditional and also help it to stand out from the crowd. Making up new spellings for a traditional name can also become trendy and quickly generate a new name craze. The name Chloe has seen a modern change in how it is spelled with some parents opting to spell the name with a 'K,' Khloe. Swapping the 'c' with a 'k' has become a popular choice for parents as these letters are easily substitutable with one and other.

Changing or mixing up the vowels, A, E, I, O, U & sometimes Y can create a brand new version of a traditional name. Very occasionally will the vowel from the first letter of a name be changed, it is frequently more common for parents to change the vowels within the name.

Names with Letter C	Names with Letter K
Cameron	Kamron
Carly	Karlee
Cailyn	Kailyn
Caitlyn	Katelyn
Cassandra	Kassandra
Catalina	Katalina
Chloe	Khloe
Danica	Danika
Dominic	Dominik
Eric	Erik
Jacob	Jakob
Lucas	Lukas
Mackenzie	Makenzie
Michaela	Makayla
Marcus	Markus
Nicholas	Nickolas
Zachary	Zakary

Vowel changes	
Aiden	Aidyn
Jayden	Jaiden
Lauren	Lauryn
Reagan	Regan
Zoe	Zoie

One of the most popular ways to modify a name is to add or to remove one or more of the consonants within the name.

Some parents decide to spell their babies name differently from the traditional way as a way to indicate the gender of their child's name. This is particularly common with baby girl names. Adding or removing consonants can create a whole new vibrant name.

There are no set rules on how to spell a name, however being creative with a name's spelling can cause problems in the long run, constantly having to correct people on spellings and pronunciations, which could also cause confusion and embarrassment throughout your child's life.

Adding or removing consonants	
Alana	Alannah
Austin	Austyn
Ava	Avah
Eliana	Elianna
Giselle	Gisselle
Hannah	Hanna
Isabelle	Izabelle
Jackson	Jaxson
Jason	Jayson
Liliana	Lillianna
Madison	Maddison

Destination Names

Destination names may have depth and personal meaning to the parents who choose to give them to their children. The name might tell a personal adventure or a story as well as being exotic and unusual. A destination name could be a destination where the couple first met or dated, where they grew up, or where the child was conceived. It could just be a location loved by the parents from a holiday or somewhere that they have always wanted to visit or live. Destination names can also send out a signal that the parents are worldly travelers.

Alicia Keys and her husband Swizz Beatz named their son Egypt. Alicia said that the name was inspired by a trip and personal journey she went on while visiting Egypt. Her husband suggested that they should use the name for their baby as the holiday was such a life changing and important time for Alicia. The Beckham's famously named their first son Brooklyn after he was apparently conceived there in the late 1990's.

Parents have numerous reasons as to why they chose destination names for their children. Locations can have great significance to people's lives and history. Honoring a city, state, county or a country by giving your baby the same name is a way of telling your story and having it live on through your family tree.

Destination names	
Austin	Lourdes
Boston	Lucia
Bronx	Madison
Brooklyn	Marseille
Carolina	Montana
Catalina	Odessa
Charlotte	Orlando
Chelsea	Oxford
Dakota	Paris
Dallas	Phoenix
Denver	Savannah
Eden (Biblical Garden of Eden)	Shiloh (Biblical city)
Georgie	Sicily
Hamilton	Sonora
Houston	Troy
India	Valencia
Ireland	Venice
Kenya	Vienna
Kingston	Virginia
Lincoln	Zion (Biblical)
London	

Gender neutral names

Gender neutral names are becoming increasingly popular with modern parents. This is most likely due to the fact that there has been a substantial rise with parents who are choosing to raise their child in a gender neutral way with clothes, toys, and unisex baby names. Companies and parents are choosing to break away from the traditions and refusing to reinforce gender stereotypes that have been around for millennia.

Blake Lively and her husband Ryan Reynolds chose the name James Reynolds for their daughter in December 2014. Mila Kunis and Aston Kutcher also chose a gender neutral name for their daughter who they named Wyatt Kutcher in September 2014. Some people believe that a masculine sounding name can be a workplace advantage for the child when it is older.

Is a name truly masculine or feminine? Well, a name will always remain a name; therefore, it is whatever your child is. However, time can make a lot of difference when it comes to gender neutral names. Names that are considered unisex today such as Courtney and Casper may not have even been considered for a girl's name twenty years ago. The more creative the spelling, the more likely that the name is being used for a girl.

Modern names often start off being unisex and then gradually start being spelled differently, thus creating a female version and a male version. Names that end with –on usually imply that the name is being used for a male, whereas names ending with –ynn tend to imply that the name is being used for a female.

Names can shift from being gender neutral to male or female over time. Therefore, if you decide to pick a gender neutral name for your baby, you should be prepared for the name to eventually tilt to being associated with either a male or a female.

When should I announce the baby name?

There is no specific time or rule on when you or your partner should announce your chosen baby name.

It is a personal choice, and nobody can tell you when you can and can't do it. You should announce the baby's name when you and your partner feel comfortable and certain with your name choice. I announced my first son's name-to-be when I was seven months pregnant. However, when he was born I didn't go with the name which I had originally chosen for him. This did cause some confusion for family and friends, as I ended up giving my son a completely different name which wasn't even considered during my pregnancy. The name for my second child was chosen during pregnancy by my partner. We both really liked the name and told everybody what the baby would be called. The only thing that we changed between the pregnancy and birth of our son was the spelling of his name. This took a little longer to decide.

Some parents decide to announce their babies name during pregnancy while others prefer to wait until the baby is born. Whether you decide to announce your babies name before or after the birth, you can still have some fun with the announcement. The rise in baby showers has also seen an increase in baby name announcements. You could do this with the use of balloons, cakes or by getting everybody to play a fun guessing game and reveal the baby's name at the very end.

The power of social media has also had a great impact on announcing both pregnancy and baby names. This is because it is an easy and cheap way to make announcements which can also be fun while reaching vast amounts of people who may live all over the world.

Photography is a fun and creative way to announce the baby's name. Some mothers like to take a picture of their pregnant bellies with the chosen baby name stuck onto the belly using a name tag. Others like to place objects on top or in front of the belly that spell out the baby's name. Letter bricks are a popular choice for this method.

If you have more than one child, involving any siblings can be an extremely fun and adorable way to announce the babies name to the world. You could have your child wearing a T-shirt with the baby's name exhibited on the front; they could be holding up a picture with the baby's name spelled out on a chalkboard, easel painting, box, or even on a tablet device. There any many creative ways that you and your family could do this.

Video announcements have seen a rise in baby name announcements. Parents are opting to use this method to announce their baby's name, the reasons behind their choice and then explaining the meaning of the name. A video announcement could also make a great family keepsake; you could watch the video together in ten or twenty years' time when your child is all grown up and maybe have some children of their own. It's a good way to look back and remember those special family moments.

A new and rising trend with parents are for them to reserve the baby's full name on social media sites, then revealing the name to family and friends with a scan picture of their newborn baby. The pages are then used to update the child's milestones with close friends and family.

Keepsake announcements have a more traditional feeling to them and can be a great keepsake for your family and friends. This can be done by using paper or card announcements with a picture of your baby, weight and size and, of course, the baby's full name.

Decorations and baby nurseries can be a good way to announce the baby's name, with the use of personalised toys, decoration stickers, wall hangers, and door names.

Being creative with food is a fun choice since buying personalised sweets and candy bars has become easier and, therefore, a fun way to make pregnancy and baby name announcements. You could combine this option with the use of photography and social media. Spelling out your baby's name with candy, alphabet spaghetti or other food items, while creating cool and artistic photographs that would make a lovely family keepsake.

The number of parents who are choosing to have a baby naming ceremony to reveal their children's full name has tripled in the past few years. With loved ones gathered together for a non-religious celebration, the name is then presented to family and friends.

Past Trends

Important titles, names which carry a grand sense of importance such as King, Queen, Prince, and Princess have been a highly popular name choice throughout the times. Although these names tended to decline during the 1950's, there has been a recent surge in popularity; this is probably because of the celebrities who are choosing these names for their own children.

'Y' spellings

Replacing a letter in the name with the letter 'y' has been a popular choice since the early twentieth century. During the 1920's it also became highly desirable to add an 'e' to names that already ended with the letter 'y' for example, Bettye, Bobbye and Rubye.

Gems

For centuries valuable gems and precious stones have been a popular choice for baby names. This includes names such as Beryl, Diamond, Opal, Pearl, and Ruby. Other signs of preciousness such as

Coral and Goldie have also been a fashionable name choice.

Boy names for girls

Choosing traditional male names and using them as female names became trendy during the late 19th century. The most popular boy's names that were given to girls are Billie, Bobbie, Charlie, Frankie, and Tommie.

Last names for first names

Last names for first names have also been a trendy option for parent's. The names Coleman, Hilton, Preston, Scott, and Spencer are just some of the names that emerged after it became increasingly popular to use surnames as given first names.

A-Z

Baby Boy Names For

2017

Aaden

Pronunciation: Ay-din.

The name originates from Irish Gaelic; it is a variant of the name Aidan. The name means, "fire," "fiery."

Aamir

Pronunciation: Aa-mir

Aamir is a modernised counterpart of the Arabic and Hebrew name Amir, which means "treetop."

Aaron

Pronunciation: Aa-ron

The name Aaron is of Greek origin. The name is also linked to Ancient Egypt. Aaron is a biblical name and appears in the Old Testament borne by the brother of Moses. The name Aaron means "Strong mountain."

Abdul

Pronunciation: AB-dul

The name Abdul is of Arabic origin and means "servant of God", "servant". The name Abdul also signifies a religious service and devotion.

Abdullah

Pronunciation: Ab-dul-ah

Abdullah is of Arabic origin and means "God's servant".

Abraham

Pronunciation: Ay-bra-ham, Ahb-rahm

The name Abraham comes from the Hebrew av haomon goyim. The name Abraham means, "Father of a multitude," "many nations." Abraham is a biblical name; borne in the Old Testament and originally named Abram, was bestowed the name of Abraham by God. He is said to be the father of Jewish nations, the great Jewish patriarchs. Abraham received God's promise that his people would possess the land of Canaan.

Abran

Pronunciation: a-BRAHN

Abran originates from Spain and means, "father of a mighty nation", "father of a multitude", "high father". Abran is a variant of the Hebrew name Abraham.

Ace

Pronunciation: Ayce

Ace is of English origin and also has an English surname meaning "Noble." The name Ace means, "Number one." Additionally, an ace is a playing card with the highest face value in many card games, making the ace the most powerful card to hold.

Achilles

Pronunciation: ah-KILL-eez

Achilles is of Greek origin. Achilles was the son of the sea nymph Thetis and Peleus, King of the Myrmidons. Achilles was a hero of the Trojan War, the central character and a supreme warrior in Homer's Iliad. Famous for his courage and manly beauty, Achilles was invulnerable on all of his body except for his heel. Achilles was dipped in the River Styx by his mother Thetis; she held him by the heel which became his one weak point, "Achilles' Heel."

Adair
Pronunciation: ah-DARE
The name Adair is of German origin. The meaning of the name Adair is, "wealthy spear". Adair is also a Scottish surname from the Gaelic word 'doire', which means "oak grove."

Adam
Pronunciation: AD-am
Adam is of Hebrew origin and means "earth." In Hebrew, it is a generic word for "man". Adam is a biblical name; borne in the Old Testament by the father of the human race, he was the first man created from the red earth of Eden by God. Adam and Eve were the first humans and lived in the Garden of Eden until they committed sin.

Adan
Pronunciation: ah-DAHN
The name Adan is of Spanish origin and is a variant of the Hebrew name Adam. The name Adan has the meaning of "earth", "fire". In Spanish, the meaning of the name Adan is "from the red earth".

Adolfo
Pronunciation: ah-DOLE-foh
The name Adolfo is a Latin name. The Latin meaning of Adolfo is "noble wolf", "majestic wolf". Additionally, Adolfo is a Spanish and Italian variant of the German name, Adolf.

Adrian
Pronunciation: Ay-dree-an
Adrian is of Latin origin; the name is derived from the Latin name "Hadrianus". The meaning of the name Adrian is "from Hadria", a town in northern Italy which gave its name to the Adriatic Sea. Adrian is also the name of several early Christian saints and Martyrs.

Agustin
Pronunciation: ah-goos-teen
Agustin has Latin origins. The Latin meaning of Agustin is "deserving of respect". Agustin is a popular Spanish name. The Spanish meanings of Agustin are "majestic", "great".

Aidan
Pronunciation: AY-den
Aidan is of Irish Gaelic origins. The meaning of Aidan is "fire". Aidan is the name of several early Irish saints, one of whom established the greatest centers of learning of its time, the monastery of Lindisfarne which is also known as The Holy Island of Lindisfarne.

Ainsley
Pronunciation: AYNS-lee
The name Ainsley is of Old English origin. The meaning of the name is "clearing", "only hermitage wood". Originally a place name Annesley or Ansley.

Alan
Pronunciation: AL-an
The name Alan is of Celtic origin. In Celtic, the meaning of the name Alan is, "noble", "harmony", "stone". The name could also

be derived from the Gaelic name 'Ailin', which means "little rock." Alan was originally a saint's name and was reborn in Britain during the Normal Conquest.

Alasdair
Pronunciation: AL-as-dare
Alasdair is of Greek origin. In Greek, the meaning of the name Alasdair is "defender", "protector of mankind". Other variations of the name include Alastair, Alistair, Allaster.

Albert
Pronunciation: AL-burt
Albert is a Norman French name of German Origin. The meaning of the name is "noble", "bright". The name was brought to England by the Normans and replaced the Old English name, Ethelbert.

Albin
Pronunciation: AL-bin
The name Albin is taken from the Latin name Albinus derived from 'albus'. The meaning of Albin is "white", "pale-skinned" Albin is also a variant of the name 'Alban'.

Alexander
Pronunciation: al-ek-ZAN-der
The name Alexander is of Greek origin, taken from the Latin form of the Greek name 'alexandros'. The meaning of Alexander is "man's defender", "warrior". Alexander appears in the Bible as the one who helps Jesus bear the cross on the journey to Calvary.

Alexis
Pronunciation: a-LEX-iss
Alexis is of Greek origin and means "defender." The name is often used a shortened variation of the name Alexander. Although Alexis is traditionally a male name, it is now also used for girls in the modern world. Saint Alexis was a popular saint of Edessa, admired as a 'man of God.'

Alfonso
Pronunciation: al-FON-so
Alfonso is of Spanish and Italian origin. The name Alfonso is a variant of the German word, 'Alphonse' which means "ready for battle." The Spanish meaning of the name Alfonso is "eager for war".

Alfred
Pronunciation: AL-fred
The name Alfred is of Anglo-Saxon origin and means, "name of a king."

Ali
Pronunciation: ah-LEE
Ali is of Arabic origin. Borne by a cousin the prophet of Muhammad, was also known as the first male convert to Islam. The name Ali is also borne by the hero in 'Ali Baba and the Forty Thieves'. The meaning of the name Ali is "excellent", "noble".

Alton
Pronunciation: ALL-tun
Alton is of English origin. The meaning of the name is "old town".

Alvin
Pronunciation: AL-vin
Alvin is of English origin. The meaning of the name is "friend", "magical being".

Amos
Pronunciation: AYM-oss
The name Amos is of Hebrew origin. The meaning of the name is, "to carry", "carried". A biblical name; borne by one of the twelve minor prophets of the Old Testament, who wrote the Book of Amos. It is the oldest of the prophetic books.

Andrew
Pronunciation: AN-droo
The name Andrew is of Greek origin, from the root andr-, 'man' giving the meaning "manly", "strong" or "Warrior". English form of the Greek name Andreas. A biblical name; borne by one of the first of Jesus's disciples, the first chosen of the 12 Apostles. Saint Andrew is the patron saint of Scotland, Greece, and Russia. His feast day is 30th November.

Angel
Pronunciation: AIN-jel
The name Angel is of Greek origin. The meaning of the name Angel is "messenger of God". A biblical name; borne as the name for the spirit creatures sent to man by God as his messengers. Angel is used for

both female and male names. Derived for the Greek "angelos".

Angus
Pronunciation: ANG-guss
Angus is of Celtic origin. The meaning of Angus is "one choice", "one strength". Angus is the anglicised form of the Irish and Scottish Gaelic name Aonghus. In Celtic mythology, Angus Og is a god of love and beauty. Angus is both a first name and surname.

Anthony
Pronunciation: AN-tha-nee
Anthony is of Latin origin, adopted from the Roman family name Antonius. The 'h' was introduced in the 17th century. Ruler of the Roman Empire and lover of Cleopatra, Marcus Antonius (82-30BC) was an early bearer of the name. Saint Anthony was an Egyptian hermit monk renowned for his resistance to the devil and founded the first Christian monastic order.

Apollo
Pronunciation: er-POH-loh
The name Apollo is of Greek origin. The name comes from Apollyon, Greek translation of the Hebrew word "Abaddon". The meaning of the name is "destroyer". A biblical name; borne as one of the early Christian disciples. The name Apollo has come to symbolise the classical and intellectual aspects of thought.

Archer
Pronunciation: AR-cher

Archer is of Latin origin, derived from the Latin arcus meaning "bow." Archer is an adopted English surname from medieval times, originally an occupational name for a skilled archer.

Archibald
Pronunciation: Ar-chi-bald
Archibald is of Old French and Old German origin. The name Archibald means "genuine," "bold," "brave." The name is particularly popular in Scotland.

Arden
Pronunciation: ARD-en
The name Arden is of Latin origin. The name means "great forest." It is the name of the magical forest in Shakespeare's "As You Like It". Arden is also the surname of Shakespeare's mother.

Ariel
Pronunciation: AR-ee-el
Ariel is of Hebrew origin. The meaning of Ariel is "lion of God". A biblical place name; used in Isaiah 29 to refer to Jerusalem. Ariel is also the scriptural name for a place in Sumeria. The name is used in literature to identify various spirits. Shakespeare gave this name to a spirit who can disappear at will in "The Tempest". Ariel is given to both male and females as a name.

Aries
Pronunciation: A-ries

The name Aries is of Latin origin. The meaning of the name is "ram". Aries is the name of the astrological sign for those born from March 21 to April 19.

Arnold
Pronunciation: AR-nold
Arnold is of Old French and Old German origin. The meaning of the name Arnold is "eagle power". A Puritan adoption, an early saint of this name was a musician at the court of Charlemagne. The name died out during the Middle Ages and was revived in the 19th Century.

Arthur
Pronunciation: AR-ther
The name Arthur is of Celtic origin. The name could have been derived from the Celtic word "artos", which means "bear." The 6th-century King Arthur and his Round Table of Knights have become renowned figures. The name was first found in the Latin form Artorius, which is of obscure origin.

Ashely
Pronunciation: ASH-lee
Ashley is an adopted surname and place name, of Old English origin. The meaning of the name Ashley is "ash meadow". Initially used as a boy's name, Ashley is now used more commonly for girl's names. Ashley is an English saint's name from the 17h century. The name was first recorded as a given name in the 16th Century. Earl of

Shaftesbury, Anthony Ashley Cooper, made the name more popular in the early 19thcentury. The humanitarian was renowned for the legislation designed to improve conditions among the working classes.

Asher
Pronunciation: ASH-er
The name Asher is of Hebrew origin. The meaning of the name Asher is "happy". A biblical name; borne as the eighth son of Jacob, was promised a life blessed with an abundance. The Puritans brought the name Asher to England.

Ashton
Pronunciation: ASH-ten
Ashton is an adopted surname of Old English origin. The meaning of the name is "ash tree town". Although the name has been used as a boy's name since the 1600's, the name is commonly given to girls.

Aston
Pronunciation: AS-ton
The name Aston is of Old English origin, and the meaning of the name is "east town", "ash tree settlement". Aston is also a place name.

Atlas
Pronunciation: AT-las
The name Atlas is of Greek origin. The meaning of Atlas is "to carry". The name bears connotations of great strength. Atlas was a mythical Titan who bore the weight of the world on his shoulders.

Auberon
Pronunciation: A(u)-be-ron
Auberon is an Old French name of Old German origin. The meaning of the name Auberon is "noble", "royal bear". The name is possibly a variation of Aubrey or Adalbero. Auberon is the king of the fairies in Shakespeare's, A Midsummer Night's Dream (1605).

August
Pronunciation: AW-gust
August is of Latin origin. The meaning of the name August is "great", "magnificent". The Latin version, Augustus is more commonly used in English-speaking countries.

Augustine
Pronunciation: AW-gus-tin
Augustine is of Latin origin. The meaning of Augustine is "great", "magnificent". Borne by perhaps the greatest of fathers of the Christian church, Saint Augustine of Hippo (354-430). Saint Augustine (sixth century) was the first Archbishop's of Canterbury, recognised for the frank "Confessions," in which he speaks, "Oh God, make me chaste – but not yet." Augustine is a diminutive of August, the English form of the Latin name Augustinus.

Augustus
Pronunciation: AW-gust-us
Augustus is of Latin origin. The meaning of Augustus is "great", "magnificent". It was given by the Senate to the Roman emperor

Octavian in 27BC. Subsequently, the name
Augustus was used by his successors. The
name was popular in the 18th century after
German princely families brought the name
to Britain.

Austin
Pronunciation: AW-sten
The name Austin is of French and Latin
origin. The name is a variation of
Augustine. The meaning of the name is
"great", "magnificent". The name was
popular in England during the 17th
Century. Saint Augustine (seventh century)
was occasionally called Austin.

Axel
Pronunciation: AX-el
Axel is of Hebrew origin. The meaning of
the name Axel is "father is peace". A
Scandinavian variant of Absalom.

Aydan
Pronunciation: AY-dan
Aydan is a variant of the Gaelic name,
Aidan, an anglicised form of the ancient
Gaelic name Aedan. The meaning of the
name Aydan is "fire".

B

Barnabas

Pronunciation: BAR-na-bus

The name Barnabas is of Greek and Aramaic origin. The meaning of Barnabas is "son of consolation". A biblical name; borne in the New Testament by Apostle who accompanied St Paul on his missionary journeys. Saint Barnabas's feast day is 11th June.

Barnaby

Pronunciation: BAR-naby

Barnaby is a medieval dialect form of the Greek, Aramaic name Barnabas. Charles Dickens popularized the name during the mid-19th century with his novel, 'Barnaby Rudge' (1841).

Baron

Pronunciation: BARE-an

The name Baron is of Old German and Old English Origin. The meaning of the name Baron is "young warrior". It is an adopted surname which was first used during the post-Conquest period to mean a vassal of a nobel. A baron was the lowest rank of a hereditary peerage that entitles the holder to serve in the House of Lords in England.

Barrett

Pronunciation: BARE-et

The name Barrett is possibly from Middle English baret, which means "dispute," "argument", or from the Old French word, Barrette meaning "cap." The adopted surname became a given name used mostly in the 19th century.

Barry

Pronunciation: BARE-ee

Barry is of Irish and Gaelic origin, derived from the Old Irish name, Bairre. The meaning of the name Barry is "fair-haired". Saint Bairre (seventh century) founded a monastery that became the city of Cork in Ireland.

Bartholomew

Pronunciation: bar-THAWL-oh-myoo

Bartholomew is of Aramaic origin. The meaning of Bartholomew is "son of Talmai". Talmai being another name for Nathaniel, the apostle. Biblical; by the name of one of the twelve apostles, Nathanael, who was known as the patron saint of tanners and vintners. Bartholomew was a common boys name in the Middle Ages.

Basil

Pronunciation: BAZ-el

The name Basil is of Greek origin. The meaning of Basil is "royal", "kingly". From the Greek name Basileios, which is derived from "basileus". Saint Basil (fourth century) of Caesarea was called "Saint Basil the Great," he was regarded as one of the Fathers of the Eastern Church. Basil is also the name of several early saints martyred in the East. The name was common in the eastern Mediterranean and was brought to England by the Crusaders. Basil is also the name of a common herb.

Beau

Pronunciation: boh

The name Beau is of French origin, and the meaning of Beau is "handsome", "sweetheart". The novel "Beau Geste" (1924) was a bestseller and a popular movie. Beau is also the name of Ashley and Melanie Wilkes child in Margaret Mitchell's legendary "Gone with the Wind" (1936).

Benedict

Pronunciation: BEN-a-dikt

Benedict is of Latin origin from the Latin word, Benedictus. The meaning of Benedict is "blessed". Saint Benedict founded the Christian monastic order, the Benedictines. The name is popular with Roman Catholics, and there has been 16 popes who have shared the name, Benedict.

Benjamin

Pronunciation: BEN-ja-men

Benjamin is of Hebrew origin, from the Hebrew name Benyamin. The meaning of Benjamin is "son of the right hand", "son of my old age". A biblical name; borne by the youngest and most beloved son of the patriarch Jacob and Rachel, who died giving birth to him. He was originally named Benoni.

Bennett

Pronunciation: BEN-et

Bennett is of French and Latin origin. The adopted surname has been used for both girl's and boy's names. Taken from the medieval vernacular form of Benedict.

Benson

Pronunciation: BEN-son

The adopted surname has been used as a given name since the 19th century. The meaning of the name Benson is "son of Ben". The name is also connected to a place name, Benson (formerly Bensington) in Oxfordshire.

Bentley

Pronunciation: BENT-lee

The name Bentley is of Old English origin. The meaning of the name Bentley is "bent grass meadow". The adopted surname is used more commonly as a boy's name. However, it is also used as a girl's name. Bentley is also a place name for many places in England.

Bernard

Pronunciation: ber-NARD

The name Bernard is of Old French and Old German origin. The meaning of the name is "strong", "brave bear". The name was brought to England by the Norman Conquest. Three famous medieval saints bore the name. An 11th century Saint Bernard of Menthon is revered as the patron saint of mountaineers. Saint Bernard of Clairvaux (1090-1153), a founder of a monastic order, and a scholastic philosopher.

Blaise

Pronunciation: blayz

The name Blaise is of French and Latin origin. From Latin Blasius, and derived from "blaesus". The meaning of the name is "lisping", "stammering". Saint Blaise, a 4th-century Armenian bishop is supposedly endowed with miraculous healing power. He is regarded as the patron of those suffering from sore throats.

Blake
Pronunciation: blayk
Blake is of Old English origin. The meaning of the name Blake is "black", "pale". The adopted surname is used as both a boy's name and a girl's name. Blake was originally used as a nickname for someone with skin or hair that was either very dark ("blaec") or very light ("blac").

Boaz
Pronunciation: boa-Z
Boaz is of Hebrew origin. A biblical name; Boaz is the name of several characters. The name was revived by the Puritans; it was occasionally used in England during the 17th and 18th centuries. The meaning of the name is "swiftness", "strength".

Boris
Pronunciation: BOR-iss
Boris is of Russian and Slavic origin. Originally from the Tartar nickname, Bogoris. The meaning of the name is "small", "battle glory". Borne by a 9th-century ruler of Bulgaria who converted his Kingdom to Christianity. A 10th-century Russian saint also known as Romanus, Saint Boris is known as the patron saint of Moscow.

Bowen
Pronunciation: BOH-en
The name Bowen is of Welsh origin. The meaning of the name Bowen is "son of Owen", "son of the young one".

Boyd
Pronunciation: boyd
Boyd is of Gaelic and Scottish origin. Boyd is an adopted Irish and Scottish surname. The name was first used as a surname in Scotland in the 13th century; it has been in regular use as a first name since the early 20th century. Scottish Gaelic, from the word buidhe, which means "yellow," "blonde."

Braden
Pronunciation: BRAY-den
The name Braden is of Irish and Gaelic origin. The meaning of the name is "descendant of bradán". Bradán is a personal name that means "salmon." Braden is an adoptive Irish surname.

Bradley
Pronunciation: BRAD-lee
Bradley is of Old English origin. The meaning of Bradley is "broad meadow", "broad wood". Bradley is an adopted surname and also a place name. Bradley has been used as a given first name since the mid-19th century.

Brady
Pronunciation: BRAY-dee

The name Brady is of Irish and Gaelic origin. The meaning of the name is "descendant of Brádach". The name is used as both a boy's name and as a girl's names.

Brandon
Pronunciation: BRAN-den
Brandon is of Old English origin. The meaning of the name Brandon is "broom", "hill". Brandon is an adopted surname and an English Place name.

Braxton
Pronunciation: b-rax-ton
Braxton is of Old English origin. The meaning of Braxton is "Brock's town". Brock is an informal word used for "badger". Braxton is an adopted surname and a place name.

Brendan
Pronunciation: BREN-den
Brendan is of Celtic, Irish, and Gaelic origin. The meaning of the name Brendan is "Prince". From an old Irish Gaelic name Bréanainn. The name was borne by a legendary 6th-century Irish abbot and saint. Saint Brendan of Ireland is renowned for his adventurous traveling and scholarship. He was known as "the Voyager" after a seven-year voyage, possibly to North America.

Brennan
Pronunciation: BREN-an
Brennan is of Irish and Gaelic origin. The meaning of the name Brennan is "Teardrop". Brennan is used as both a

boy's name and as a girl's name. The name is also a variant of Brendan.

Brent
Pronunciation: brent
The name Brent is of Old English and Celtic origin. The meaning of the name is "Hill", "mount". The name might also have been used to refer to criminals branded or burned as a punishment. Brent is an adopted surname.

Brenton
Pronunciation: BREN-ton
Brenton is of Old English origin. The meaning of Brenton is "Bryni's settlement". Brenton is also an adopted surname and a place name.

Brett
Pronunciation: bret
The name Brett is of Latin origin. The meaning of the name is "from Britany", "from Britain". Brett is an adopted surname which originated in the Middle Ages, as an ethnic name for a native of Brittany.

Brian
Pronunciation: BRY-en
The name Brian is of Celtic, Irish, and Gaelic origin. The meaning of the name Brian is "high", "noble". The name was possibly introduced to England by Norman invaders; however, the name was born by a great Irish chieftain, Brian Boroimhe. He was a warrior who became the high king of Ireland and one of its greatest national

heroes. After he defeated a Viking invasion and liberated the country from the Danes in 1014.

Broderick
Pronunciation: BRAH-der-ik
Broderick is a transferred use of the surname, which is derived from the Welsh personal name Rhydderch. The name could be of Old German origin and mean, "famous power."

Brody
Pronunciation: BROH-dee
The name Brody is of Irish and Gaelic origin. The meaning of Brody is "ditch". Brody is also a place name; there is a Castle Brodie in Scotland. It could also possibly be related to "brathair" which means, "brother" in Irish.

Brooks
Pronunciation: brux
Brooks is of Old English and Old German origin. The meaning of Brooks is "water", "small stream". Brooks is used as both a boy's name and a girl's name.

Bruce
Pronunciation: brooce
Bruce is of Norman-French origin, introduced to Britain by the Norman Conquest. Adopted Scottish surname, originally a Norman baronial name and place name.

Bruno
Pronunciation: BROO-noh
The name Bruno is of Old German origin. From Old German brun, the meaning of the name Bruno is "brown". Bruno was used as a name in the ruling families of Germany during the Middle Ages. Saint Bruno was a 10th-century German saint who founded an order of Carthusian monks, whom the German town of Brunswick is named.

Bryn
Pronunciation: br-yn
The name Bryn is of Welsh origin. The meaning of the name Bryn is "hill". The name is also a short form of Brynmor. Bryn is used as both a boy's name and a girl's name.

Bryce
Pronunciation: Bryce
The name Bruce is of Scottish origin. The meaning of Bryce is "of Britain". Bryce is a variant of Brice which originated as a transferred use of the Scottish surname, derived from the medieval given name.

Buddy
Pronunciation: bud-DEE
Buddy is a variant of the English word Bud. The meaning of Buddy is "brother", and it has been used as a nickname since the medieval times.

Byron

Pronunciation: BYE-ron

Byron is an adopted surname and English place name derived from byre, "barn", "cowshed". The name is of Old English origin. The meaning of Byron is "at the byres". The name was popular in the 19th century. Lord Byron was a poet renowned for his wildness and debauchery.

C

Caddis
Pronunciation: CAD-is
The name Caddis is of Old English origin.
The meaning of Caddis is "worsted fabric".

Cade
Pronunciation: kayd
The name Cade is of Old English and Old
French origin. The meaning of the name
Cade is "round", "gentle cask". The
adopted surname was originally used as a
nickname. Cade was also the name of a
character in Margaret Mitchell's, "Gone
with the Wind" (1936).

Caden
Pronunciation: KAY-den
Caden is of Scottish origin, taken from the
Scottish surname McCadden. The meaning
of the name is "son of Cadán."

Cadogan
Pronunciation: ca-do-gan
Cadogan is of Welsh origin. Anglicised
form of Cadwgan or cadwgawn, derived
from cad, meaning "battle," gwogann,
meaning "glory." The meaning of the name
Cadogan is "battle glory". It is the name of
several Welsh princes from the early
Middle Ages. Borne by two characters in
Mabinogian, the collection of Welsh
legends.

Caesar
Pronunciation: SEE-zer
The name Caesar is of Latin origin. The
meaning of Caesar is "head of hair". A
famous bearer of the name was Roman
Emperor Julius Caesar (104-44BC). Julius

Caesar, which was traditionally said to be
derived from caesus, 'cut.' Cut from his
dead mother's womb; Caesar was the first
baby to have been delivered by Caesarean
section. Due to his success and power, the
name Caesar then became the title of the
Roman emperors with the meaning "ruler".

Caius
Pronunciation: keys
The name Caius is of Latin origin. The
meaning of Caius is "happy". The name is
a common Roman form of the name Gaius.

Caiden
Pronunciation: KAY-den
The name Caiden is of Arabic origin. The
name may also refer to an Old English
word meaning "round." The name Caiden
means "companion." It is also a variant of
the name Kaden.

Cain
Pronunciation: KA-yn
The name Cain is of Hebrew origin. The
meaning of Cain is "acquired, spear". A
Biblical name; Cain was Adam and Eve's
first born son. He killed his brother in
anger and jealousy, and he spent the rest of
his life as a wanderer in exile.

Cairo
Pronunciation: KIE-ro
Cairo is of Arabic origin. The meaning of
the name is "victorious". Cairo is also a
place name, the capital of Egypt.

Caleb
Pronunciation: KAY-leb

Caleb is of Hebrew origin. The meaning of the name Caleb is "faith, whole-hearted". A biblical name; a companion of Moses and Joshua. Caleb was noted for his fearlessness and his devotion to God. The name was popular among the Puritans.

Callan

Pronunciation: KAL-an

The name Callan is of Gaelic and Scottish origin. The meaning of Callan is "battle, rock". Callan is originally a surname.

Callum

Pronunciation: KAL-um

Callum is of Scottish Gaelic origin. The name is a variant of Calum. Derived from the Latin first name Columba, meaning 'dove.' Borne by an early Celtic saint (521-597).

Calvin

Pronunciation: KAL-vin

The name Calvin is of French origin. The meaning of Calvin is "little bald one". An adopted French surname, from Old French chauve, 'bald'. Given at first in honour of the French theologian Jean Calvin (1509-1564).

Camden

Pronunciation: KAM-den

The name Camden is of Scottish and Gaelic origin. The meaning of the name Camden is "winding valley." Camden is also a place name.

Cameron

Pronunciation: KAM-er-en

Cameron is of Scottish and Gaelic origin. The meaning of Cameron is "crooked nose, crooked stream". Cameron is used as both a boy's name and as a girl's name. The adopted Scottish surname was borne by a prominent Highland clan. The name was rarely used outside of Scotland before the 1950's.

Camilo

Pronunciation: ka-MEE-loh

Camilo is of Latin origin. The meaning of the name Camilo is "helper to the priest". The name is a masculine variation of the name Camilla.

Campbell

Pronunciation: CAM-bel

Campbell is of Scottish and Gaelic origin. An adopted Scottish surname, from cam beaul. The meaning of the name Campbell is "crooked mouth". A family name of the Dukes of Argyll. The name has been in use since the mid-20th century.

Carl

Pronunciation: karl

The name Carl is of Old German origin. The name Carl is an old fashioned variation of Karl, the German form of Charles.

Carlos

Pronunciation: KAR-lohs

Carlos is of Spanish origin. The meaning of the name Carlos is "free man". The name is a variant of the name Charles.

Carlton
Pronunciation: KARL-ten
The name Carlton is of Old English origin. The meaning of Carlton is "free peasant settlement". Adopted surname and common English place name, from Old English carl.

Carson
Pronunciation: KAR-sen
Carson is of Scottish and Old English origin. The meaning of the name Cason is "son of the marsh-dwellers". Carson is an adopted Scottish surname, possibly taken from the medieval name de Carsan. The first known bearer was Robert de Carsan in the 13th century.

Carter
Pronunciation: KAR-ter
Carter is of Old English origin. The meaning of the name Carter is "one who transports goods". Originally a surname and a given occupational name.

Casey
Pronunciation: KAY-see
The name Casey is of Irish and Gaelic origin. The meaning of Casey is "alert, watchful". The name Casey is used as both a boy's name, and as a girl's name. Casey is from the Gaelic male name Cathasaigh.

Cassius
Pronunciation: KASH-us
Cassius is of Latin origin. The meaning of the name Cassius is "empty, hollow". The name is an old Roman family clan name.

Cecil
Pronunciation: SESS-ul
The name Cecil is of Latin origin. The meaning of Cecil is "blind". An adopted surname from the Roman family name Caecilius, derived from Latin Caecus, 'blind'. The name was popular during the late 19th century.

Cedric
Pronunciation: SED-rik
The name Cedric is of Old English origin. The meaning of Cedric is "kind, loved". Possibly an altered form of the name Cerdic, a 6th-century king of Wessex. The name Cedric was invented by Sir Walter Scott for the character Cedric of Rotherwood for his book, Ivanhoe (1819).

Cesar
Pronunciation: sez-ZAR
Cesar is of Latin origin. The meaning of the name Cesar is "head of hair".

Chance
Pronunciation: chans
The name Chance is of Middle English origin. The meaning of Chance is "good fortune". Originally a surname. Chance is also a variant of the name Chauncey.

Chandler
Pronunciation: CHAND-ler
Chandler is of Middle English and Old French origin. The meaning of the name Chandler is "candle maker". The adopted surname was also an occupational name from 'chandele' meaning 'candle'. Chandler is used as both a boy's name and as a girl's name.

Charles
Pronunciation: charlz
Charles is of Old German origin. The meaning of the name Charles is "free man". Charles the Great (742-814) was also known as Charlemagne, was a powerful German leader who created a more ordered society out of the chaos that followed the fall of Rome. Charles became king of the Franks in 771; he was the first Holy Roman Emperor in 800. He united France and much of central Europe. He was said to have been eight feet tall and extremely strong. His widespread fame gave rise to many forms of his name. Charles and its variant forms have been favored by royalty of several different countries. Diminutives: Charley, Charlie, Chas, Chay, Chuck.

Chester
Pronunciation: CHES-ter
Chester if of Old English and Latin origin. The meaning of the name Chester is "camp of soldiers". Chester is an adopted surname and English place name that is derived from Latin castra, 'camp'.

Chris
Pronunciation: kris
The name Chris is of Greek origin. The meaning of Chris is "bearing Christ". Chris is a short form of the names Christopher and Christian.

Christian
Pronunciation: KRIS-chen
Christian is of Latin origin. The meaning of the name Christian is "follower of Christ". According to the Bible, the term was first used at Antioch (Acts 11:26); 'And when he had found him, he brought him unto Antioch. And the disciples were called Christians first in Antioch'. The name Christian comes from the Latin girl's name, Christianus. It may have become a popular male name due to the success of John Bunyan's 'Pilgrim's Progress' (1678), whose hero is called Christian. Diminutives: Chris, Christie, Christy.

Christopher
Pronunciation: KRIS-toh-fer
Christopher is of Greek origin. The meaning of the name Christopher is "bearing Christ". From the Greek name Khristophoros, from Khristos. The name was popular among early Christians. The symbolic legend of giant Saint Christopher, 'the bearer of Christ', carried the Christ child safely across a river. Saint Christopher is considered the patron saint of travelers. The name has been in constant use since

the 15th century. Diminutives: Chris, Kris, Christie, Kester, Christy.

Cian

Pronunciation: KEE-an

The name Cian is of Irish and Gaelic origin. The meaning of Cian is "ancient". Borne by the name of Brian Boru's son in law, who played a major role in the battle of Clontarf in the 11th century.

Clarence

Pronunciation: KLARE-ence

Clarence is of Latin origin. The meaning of Clarence is "one who lives near the river Clare". Clarence was first used as a given name since the mid-19th century.

Clark

Pronunciation: klark

The name Clark is of Latin origin. The meaning of Clark is "clerk, cleric". An adopted surname, originally an occupational name for a clerk or cleric. The name was popularized in the 20th century by the actor Clark Gable (1901-1960). The name was also made famous by the fictional character Clark Kent, otherwise known as Superman.

Clay

Pronunciation: KLAY

Clay is of Old English origin. Originally an occupational or place name which involved clay. Clay was a valued natural resource in earlier times. Clay can be used as a short form of the name Clayton.

Clayton

Pronunciation: KLAYT-en

The name Clayton is of Old English origin. The meaning of Clayton is "clay settlement". The name is an adopted surname and English place name derived from Clay. Its use as a first name dates back to the beginning of the 19th century.

Clement

Pronunciation: KLEM-ent

Clement is of Latin origin. The meaning of the name Clement is "merciful". Borne by several early saints, including Clement of Alexandria (c.150-c215). A disciple of St Paul who became the first of thirteen popes bearing the name. The name was popular during the Middle Ages.

Clifford

Pronunciation: KLIF-erd

The name Clifford is of Old English origin. The meaning of Clifford is "cliff-side ford". Originally a surname used as given name from the seventh-century. Diminutive; Cliff.

Clifton

Pronunciation: KLIF-ten

The name Clifton is of Old English Origin. The meaning of Clifton is "town by the cliff". Originally a surname used as a given name.

Clinton

Pronunciation: KLIN-ten

Clinton is of Old English origin. The

meaning of Clinton is "fenced settlement".
Clinton is both a surname and a place name
from Glympton, in Oxfordshire.

Clive
Pronunciation: kleeve
The name Clive is of Old English origin.
The meaning of Clive is "cliff, slope". Clive
is an adopted surname and place name
from Old English Clif. The name was made
popular in honor of Robert Clive, a famous
English soldier known as Clive of India.

Clyde
Pronunciation: klyd
The name Clyde is of Scottish origin. Clyde
is also a place name, the River Clyde in
Scotland. Clyde Barrow was a notorious
outlaw, who made the name well known
during The Great Depression with his
partner Bonnie.

Cody
Pronunciation: KO-dee
The name Cody is of Irish and Gaelic
origin. The meaning of the name Cody is
"helper". Cody is used as both a boy's
name, and as a girl's name.

Cole
Pronunciation: kohl
Cole is of Middle English and Old French
origin. The meaning of Cole is "charcoal".
Originally a surname that was derived from
a medieval given name. Cole is used as both
a boy's name and, as a girl's name.

Colin
Pronunciation: KOH-lin
Colin is of Irish and Scottish Gaelic origin.
The meaning of the name is "young
creature". The name has been used as an
Anglicised form of Cailean. Collin is a
diminutive form of the medieval name
Colle, which is a short form of the Greek
name Nicholas.

Conan
Pronunciation: KOH-nan
Conan is of English, Irish and Scottish
Gaelic origin. The meaning of Conan is
"hound, high". The name was taken to
Ireland after the Norman Conquest. Borne
in Irish legend, Conan was a warrior who
fought under Finn Mac Fumhail (Finn
McCool). Also the name of a seventh-
century saint who was an Irish missionary
on the Isle of Man.

Connor
Pronunciation: KAH-ner
Connor is of Irish and Gaelic origin.
Anglicised form of the Irish Gaelic name
Conchobhar, borne in Irish legend by the
son of Nessa, who became a legendary king
of Ulster. As an old man, he lusted after the
young Deirdre and forced her to marry
him. The meaning of Connor is "hound-
lover".

Conrad
Pronunciation: KAHN-rad

Conrad is of Old German origin. The
meaning of Conrad is "brave, counsel". The
name of the 10th-century bishop of
Constance, it was reintroduced to the
English-speaking world in the 19th century.
Conrad is also the name of nine saints and
several German kings during the Middle
Ages.

Constantine
Pronunciation: KAHN-stan-teen
Constantine is of Latin origin. The meaning
of Constantine is "constant". Constantine
the Great (c. 288-337) was the first Cristian
emperor, who left Rome to found
Constantinople. The name was popular
among the Puritans as a virtue name.
Constantine was also the name of 11
Byzantine emperors and a royal name in
Greece. Borne by three Scottish kings.

Cooper
Pronunciation: KOO-per
The name Cooper is of Old English origin.
The meaning of Cooper is "barrel maker".
The name may also be the English form of a
German surname which means
"coppersmith."

Corey
Pronunciation: KOR-ee
The name Corey is an English surname
derived from an Old Norse personal name
Kori. Corey is used as both a boy's name,
and as a girl's name. The meaning of the
name may mean "God, peace."

Cornelius
Pronunciation: kor-NEEL-yus
The name Cornelius is of Latin origin. The
Roman family name may be derived from
cornu. The meaning of Cornelius is "horn".
Cornelius is a famous Latin clan name. A
biblical name: borne by a Roman centurion
converted by St Peter. Cornelius is also the
name of a third-century pope who is
venerated as a saint.

Cortez
Pronunciation: kor-TEZ
Cortez is of Spanish origin. The meaning of
the name Cortez is "courteous". The name
is also a variant of Curtis. Cortez was the
surname of the 16th-century Spanish
explorer Hernando Cortes. His small
expeditionary force conquered the Aztec
civilization of Mexico.

Courtney
Pronunciation: COURT-ney
Courtney is of Old French origin. The
meaning of Courtney is "domain of
Curtis". The name is both a surname and a
place name. Courtney is a Norman baronial
name from places in Northern France
called Courtenay. Courtney is used as both
a boy's name and a girl's name.

Craig
Pronunciation: krayg
Craig is of Scottish and Gaelic origin. The
meaning of Craig is "Rocky". The name is
derived from the word "crag". Originally
Craig was used as a Scottish surname.

Cruz

Pronunciation: Krooz

Cruz is of Spanish and Portuguese origin.
The meaning of the name Cruz is "cross."

Curtis

Pronunciation: KERT-iss

The name Curtis is of English and Old
French origin. The meaning of Curtis is
"Courteous, polite". Originally used as a
nickname in the Middle Ages, for a
courteous person. Curtis is also used as a
surname. Curtis was originally used as a
first name in the 19th century.

Cyrus

Pronunciation: SY-russ

Cyrus is of Greek origin. The meaning of
Cyrus is "Lord". Derived from Kyros of the
name of several kings of Persia. A biblical
name; Cyrus is named in the book of Isaiah,
as the one who would overthrow Babylon
and liberate the Israelites. In the fifth
century BC, Cyrus the Great conquered
Babylon at the height of its powers and
founded the Persian Empire.

D

Dace

Pronunciation: dayce

The name Dace is of French origin. The meaning of Dace is "of the nobility". The name may also be used as a form of Dasius and Datius.

Dacey

Pronunciation: DAY-cee

Dacey is of Irish, Gaelic and Latin origin. The meaning of Dacey is "from the South". The name is used as both a boy's name and as a girl's name.

Dag

Pronunciation: dag

Dag is of Scandinavian origin. The meaning of the name Dag is "daylight". Borne in mythology; Dag was the son of Night who brought the daylight as he rode his horse around the earth.

Dagan

Pronunciation: DAY-gan

The name Dagan is of Hebrew origin. The meaning of Dagan is "the earth".

Dagobert

Pronunciation: DAG-o-bert

The name Dagobert is of Old German origin. The meaning of Dagobert is "bright day".

Dahy

Pronunciation: DA-hy

Dahy is of Irish and Gaelic origin. The meaning of the name of Dahy is "quick-footed".

Dailey

Pronunciation: DAY-lee

The name Dailey is of Irish and Gaelic origin. The meaning of Dailey is "assembly".

Dainard

Pronunciation: DAYN-ard

Dainard is of Old English origin. The meaning of Dainard is "bold Dane".

Dakota

Pronunciation: da-KOH-tah

Dakota is of Native American Indian origin. The meaning of the name Dakota is "friend". Originally a tribal and place name.

Dale

Pronunciation: dayl

The name Dale is of Old English origin. The meaning of Dale is "Valley". Originally a surname, Dale is also a place name.

Dalton

Pronunciation: DOLL-ton

The name Dalton is of Old English origin. The meaning of Dalton is "from the valley town". Dalton is also a place name.

Damian

Pronunciation: DAY-mee-en

Damian is of Greek origin. The meaning of the name Damian is "to tame". Anglicised from the Greek name Damianos, from daman, 'to tame'. Saint Damian, a 4th-century Greek martyr, is known as the patron saint of doctors. The Belgian Priest

Father Damien is honoured for giving his life to the lepers of Molokai in Hawaii.

Damon

Pronunciation: DAY-mon

The name Damon is of Greek origin. The meaning of Damon is "one who Tames". From Greek demos, 'land' or 'people'. The name is a variant of Damian.

Dane

Pronunciation: dayn

Dane is of English origin. The meaning of the name Dane is "from Denmark". Originally a surname that indicated Danish ancestry.

Daniel

Pronunciation: DAN-yel

The name Daniel is of Hebrew origin. The meaning of Daniel is "God has judged". A biblical name; borne in the Old Testament by a prophet and writer, his story is told in the book of Daniel. He is probably most known for being thrown into a den of lions and surviving (Daniel 6:16). Diminutives: Dan, Dannie, Danny

Danny

Pronunciation: DANN-ee

Danny is of Hebrew origin. The meaning of the name Danny is "God has judged". Danny is a variant of the name Daniel.

Dante

Pronunciation: DAHN-tay

Dante is of Spanish, Latin, and Italian origin. The meaning of the name Dante is "lasting, enduring". Poet, Dante Alighieri was best known for Dante's Inferno, his graphic description of the medieval version of Hell.

Danyal

Pronunciation: DAN-yal

The name Danyal is of Hebrew origin. The meaning of Danyal is "God has judged". Danyal is a variant of the name Daniel.

Darcy

Pronunciation: DAR-cee

The name Darcy is of Irish and Gaelic origin. The meaning of Darcy is "dark". An adopted Norman baronial surname (D'Arcy). The name was introduced to Britain during the Norman Conquest. Darcy is used as both a boy's name, and as a girl's name. Darcy is also a Norman place name.

Dargan

Pronunciation: DAR-gan

The name Dargan is of Irish origin. The meaning of Dargan is "black haired". The name is a variant of Deegan.

Darius

Pronunciation: DARE-ee-us

The name Darius is of Greek and Persian origin. The meaning of Darius is "maintains possessions well". From the Greek name Dareios, derived from Old Persian darayavush, from daraya, 'posses', and vahu, 'well'. A biblical name; born in the Old Testament by Darius the Great. He was the governor of Persia, who became king in 521BC (Ezra 4:5). Darius is also the name of a saint, who was martyred at Nicaea.

Darrell

Pronunciation: DARR-ell

The name Darrell is of Old English and Old French origin. The meaning of Darrell is "open". An adopted surname and originally a French place name, Arielle in the northern region of Calvados. Darrell is also a variant of the name Darryl.

Darren

Pronunciation: DAR-en

Darren is of Irish and Gaelic origin. The meaning of the name Darren is "great". Originally an adopted Irish surname first used as a given name in the 20th century. The name became popular during the 1960's.

Dave

Pronunciation: DAY-ve

The name Dave is of Hebrew origin. The meaning of Dave is "beloved; son of David". Dave is a variant of the name David.

David

Pronunciation: DAY-vid

The name David is of Hebrew origin. The meaning of David is "beloved". From Hebrew dawid, which means 'beloved.' A biblical name; borne in the Old Testament by the youngest son of Jesse. David was a shepherd, poet, musician, soldier, king and a prophet. He slew the giant Goliath and found favor with Saul with his talented harp playing. He is the only David mentioned in the Bible. The 6th-century saint, St David is regarded as patron saint of Wales. Diminutives: Dave, Davey, Davy.

Dawson

Pronunciation: DAW-sun

The name Dawson is of Old English origin. The meaning of Dawson is "son of David". Originally a form of the medieval surname.

Deacon

Pronunciation: DEE-ken

Deacon is of Greek origin. The meaning of the name Deacon is "Dusty one; messenger". A deacon is a ministerial assistant in a Christian congregation.

Dean

Pronunciation: deen

Dean if of Old English origin. The meaning of the name Dean is "Valley". An adopted surname, derived from the Old English denu, meaning 'valley.' Dean is also a place name.

Declan

Pronunciation: DECK-lan

The name Declan is of Irish origin. The meaning of Declan is unknown. Anglicised form of the Irish Gaelic name Deaglán. Borne by the 5th-century Irish bishop of Ardmore.

Dennis

Pronunciation: DEN-iss

Dennis is of English and Greek origin. The meaning of the name Dennis is "follower of Dionysius". The name is a variant of Dionysius. A biblical name; borne by a judge of Athens who was converted to Christianity by the Apostle Paul. A 3rd-century evangelist missionary to Gaul and a traditional patron saint of France was said to have been beheaded in Paris in 272. He was then supposed to have walked for two miles carrying his own head, before placing it down on the site which is now where the Cathedral of Saint Denis stands.

Diminutives: Dennie, Denny.

Denzil

Pronunciation: DEN-zil

The name Denzil is of Old English origin. The meaning of Denzil is unknown. An adopted surname, from Denzell, in Cornwall. It was first adopted by the Holles family when it became connected to them by marriage.

Derek

Pronunciation: DARE-ik

The name Derek is of Old German origin. The meaning of Derek is "people's ruler". The name is a German form of Theodoric. Derek was introduced to Britain in the late Middle Ages by immigrant Flemish weavers and merchants.

Desmond

Pronunciation: DEZ-mund

The name Desmond is of Gaelic and Irish origin. The meaning of Desmond is "from South Munster". Originally an adopted surname and Irish place name referring to Munster which is one of the five regions of ancient Ireland. From Irish Gaelic Deas Mumhain, which means 'South Munster.' The name was first used in Ireland in the mid-19th century.

Devon

Pronunciation: DEV-en

Devon is of English origin. The meaning of the name Devon is uncertain. Devon is originally an adopted surname, English county name, and the name of several towns in America. The name is used as both a boy's name and, as a girl's name.

Dexter

Pronunciation: DEKS-ter

The name Dexter is of Old English and Latin origin. The meaning of Dexter is "right handed, fortunate". Originally derived from Greek dexi, meaning 'worship.' Dexter is an Old English occupational name.

Diego

Pronunciation: dee-AY-go

Diego is of Spanish origin. The meaning of the name Diego is "he who supplants". Borne by a Mexican peasant to whom the Virgin of Guadalupe appeared was called Juan Diego.

Digby

Pronunciation: DIG-bee

The name Digby is of Old Norse origin. The meaning of Digby is "town by the ditch". Digby is also a place name.

Dillan
Pronunciation: DILL-an
The name Dillan is of Irish and Gaelic origin. The meaning of Dillan is "like a lion, loyal". The name is a variant of Dillon. Dillan is used as both a boy's name and, as a girl's name.

Dion
Pronunciation: DEE-on
Dion is of Greek origin. The meaning of the name Dion is unknown. Dion is a short form of the name Dionysius.

Dirk
Pronunciation: derk
The name Dirk is of Dutch origin. The meaning of the Dirk is "the people's ruler". The name is a variation of Derek. The name was made popular by a Scottish-born actor and writer, Dirk Bogarde. Dirk is also a Scottish term for a small, sharp knife.

Dominic
Pronunciation: DAH-ma-nik
Dominic is of Latin origin. The meaning of the name Dominic is "Lord". From Latin Dominicus, which means 'of the Lord.' St Dominic (1170-1221) founded the Dominican order of the monks. The name became popular throughout the Christian world. Diminutive: Dom.

Donald
Pronunciation: DAHN-ald
Donald is of Gaelic and Scottish origin. The meaning of Donald is "great chief". Anglicised form of the Scottish Gaelic name Domhall (doe-nall). From Old Celtic dubno, meaning 'world', and val, 'rule.' Donald is one of the clan names of Scotland. Borne by several early kings of Scotland. Diminutives: Don, Donny.

Donovan
Pronunciation: DAH-na-vun
The name Donovan is of Irish and Gaelic origin. The meaning of Donovan is "dark-haired chieftain".

Doran
Pronunciation: DOR-an
The name Doran is of Irish and Gaelic origin. The meaning of Doran is "stranger, exile".

Dorian
Pronunciation: DOR-ee-en
The name Dorian is of Greek origin. The meaning of Dorian is "Descendant of Dorus". Borne by an ancient Greek people and meaning 'from Doris' (an area of northern Greece). The name was popularised by Oscar Wilde's novel, The Picture of Dorian Gray (1891).

Dougal
Pronunciation: DOO-gal

The name Dougal is of Celtic origin. The meaning of Dougal is "dark stranger". Anglicised of the Irish Gaelic name Dubhghall, meaning 'dark stranger.' The name was given by the Irish to invading Vikings in the 9th century. Diminutives: Dough, Dougie.

Douglas

Pronunciation: DUG-las

The name Douglas is of Gaelic and Scottish origin. The meaning of Douglas is "black river". Initially derived from the River Douglas, the name is also a place name. The name was adopted by a powerful clan and used as a first name in the 16th century. The river name and surname is also found in Ireland, Scotland and the Isle of Man. Diminutives: Doug, Dougie.

Dudley

Pronunciation: DUD-lee

Dudley is of Old English origin. The meaning of the name Dudley is "people's field". Dudley is an adopted surname and English place name. An aristocratic family name of the Earls of Leicester. Dudley has been used as a given name since the 19th century.

Duncan

Pronunciation: DUN-kin

The name Duncan is of Gaelic and Scottish origin. The meaning of Duncan is "dark warrior". Borne by a 7th-century abbot of Iona and two medieval kings of Scotland, including Duncan I who was murdered by Macbeth in 1040. Shakespeare immortalised him in his play, Macbeth (1606).

Dunstan

Pronunciation: DUN-sten

Dunstan is of Old English origin. The meaning of Dunstan is "brown hill". From Old English dun, 'hill', and stan meaning, 'stone'. St Dunstan was a renowned 10th century Archbishop of Canterbury, who restored the monastery system in England. Dunstan is also a place name.

Dylan

Pronunciation: DIL-an

The name Dylan is of Welsh origin. The meaning of Dylan is "son of the sea". Borne in a Welsh legend by the son of a sea god. Welsh poet Dylan Thomas (1914-1953), and American singer Bob Dylan (1941) popularised the name.

E

Eamon

Pronunciation: AY-mon

Eamon is of Irish and Gaelic origin. The meaning of the name Eamon is "wealthy protector". The name is a variant of Edmund.

Earl

Pronunciation: erl

The name Earl is of Old English origin. The meaning of Earl is "nobleman, warrior". From Old English eorl. The name was originally based on the English title, and used as a nickname for people who worked for the aristocratic household of Earl.

Earland

Pronunciation: erl-AND

The name Earland is of Old English origin. The meaning of Earland is "earl's land". Earland is also a place name.

Earlston

Pronunciation: erl-ST-on

The name Earlston is of Old English origin. The meaning of Earlston is "earl's settlement".

Early

Pronunciation: erl-EE

Early is of Old English origin. The meaning of the name Early is "eagle wood". Possibly derived from the Old English term eorlic, or from the English word 'early'.

Earvin

Pronunciation: EAR-vin

The name Earvin is of Gaelic origin. The meaning of Earvin is "green, freshwater". The name is a variant of Irvin. The name was made famous by American basketball legend Earvin 'Magic' Johnson.

Eastman

Pronunciation: EES-tman

The name Eastman is of Old English origin. The meaning of Eastman is "man from the East".

Easton

Pronunciation: EES-tun

Easton is of Old English origin. The meaning of the name Easton is "East settlement". The name may have been derived from an Old English phrase meaning, 'island of stones'.

Eben

Pronunciation: EBB-an

The name Eben is of Hebrew origin. The meaning of Eben is "stone". The name is also used as a nickname for Ebenezer.

Ebenezer

Pronunciation: EBB-an-ee-zer

The name Ebenezer is of Hebrew origin. The meaning of Ebenezer is "stone of help". A biblical name; Ebenezer was the name of a memorial stone set up by the prophet Samuel to mark a critical battle and victory in Jewish history. The name was first used as a given first name in the 17th century by the Puritans. Charles Dicken's popularised the name in his novel, A Christmas Carol (1843).

Edan

Pronunciation: EE-dan

The name Edan is of Irish, Gaelic, and Scottish origin. The meaning of Edan is "fire". The name is a variant of Aidan. Edan is also a saint's name.

Edbert

Pronunciation: ED-bert

The name Edbert is of Old English origin. The meaning of Edbert is "bright".

Eddie

Pronunciation: ED-ee

Eddie is of English origin. The meaning of the name Eddie is unknown. The name is used as a nickname for Edgar, Edmund, Edward and Edwin. Eddie is used as both a boy's name and, as a girl's name.

Edel

Pronunciation: ED-el

Edel is of Old German origin. The meaning of the name Edel is "noble".

Edgar

Pronunciation: ED-gar

Edgar is of Old English origin. The meaning of the name Edgar is "spear". From the Old English name Eadgar, from ead, 'riches' or 'prosperous', and gar, 'spear'. A royal name in Anglo-Saxon England. Borne by a 10th-century king of England. Edgar is one of few early Anglo-Saxon names to have survived the Norman Conquest. Shakespeare used the name for the son of the Duke of Gloucester in King Lear (1605). Diminutives: Ed, Eddy, Eddie

Edmund

Pronunciation: ED-mund

The name Edmund is of Old English origin. The meaning of Edmund is "wealthy protector". From the Old English name Eadmund, from ead, 'rich', and mund, 'protection'. Edmund is the name of several early royal and saintly figures. The name was one of few early Anglo-Saxon names to have survived the Norman Conquest. Diminutives: Ed, Eddy, Eddie, Ned, Neddie, Neddy, Ted, Teddy, Teddie.

Edward

Pronunciation: ED-werd

Edward is of Old English origin. The meaning of the name Edward is "wealthy guard". From the Old English name Eadweard, from ead, 'rich', and weard, 'guardian'. Edward is one of the few Anglo-Saxon names to have survived the Norman Conquest. Borne by three Anglo-Saxon kings and eight kings of England since the Norman Conquest. King Edward the Confessor, 1042-1066 was also a saint. Edward is a consistently popular name. Diminutives: Ed, Eddie, Eddy, Ned, Neddy, Neddie, Ted, Teddy, Teddie.

Edwin

Pronunciation: ED-win

The name Edwin is of Old English origin. The meaning of Edwin is "wealthy friend".

From the Old English name Eadwine, from ead, 'rich', and wine, 'friend'. Borne by a 7th -century king of Northumberland who converted to Christianity. Edwin is one of the few Anglo-Saxon names to have survived the Norman Conquest. The name was revived in the 19th century. Diminutives: Ed, Eddie.

Eli
Pronunciation: EE-lye
The name Eli is of Hebrew origin. The meaning of Eli is "high". The Hebrew meaning is, "height, elevation". A biblical name; borne in the Old Testament by a high priest who brought up the prophet Samuel. The holy name was popular among Puritans in the 17th century.

Elias
Pronunciation: ee-LYE-us
Elias is of Greek and Hebrew origin. The meaning of the name Elias is "Jehovah is God". A biblical name; borne in the New Testament, from the Greek form of Elijah.

Eliot
Pronunciation: EL-i-ot
The name Eliot is of Greek and Hebrew origin. The meaning of Eliot is "Jehovah is God". The name is a variant of the biblical name, Elias. An adopted surname, diminutive of Elie. Also the Old French form of Elias.

Elroy
Pronunciation: EL-roy

Elroy is of French origin. The meaning of the name Elroy is "the king". The name is a variation of Leroy. Possibly influenced by the Spanish el, 'the'.

Elwin
Pronunciation: EL-win
The name Elwin is of Old English origin. The meaning of Elwin is "elf, fair brow". From Old English aethel, 'nobel', and wine, 'friend'. Variant of Elvin.

Elwyn
Pronunciation: EL-win
Elwyn is of Gaelic and Welsh origin. The meaning of the name Elwyn is, "white, blessed, holy". Influenced by Welsh (g)wyn. A variant of the name Alan. Elwyn is also a form of the name of a 6th-century Irish saint.

Emil
Pronunciation: AY-mul
The name Emil is of Latin origin. The meaning of Emil is "rival, eager". The German name is derived from the Latin Aemilius, meaning 'eager.'

Emile
Pronunciation: AY-mile
Emile is of Latin origin. The meaning of the name Emile is "rival, eager". The name is a variant of Emil. From the Roman surname Aesmilius. The name was made popular by the French writer Emile Zola (1840-1902).

Emanuel
Pronunciation: ee-MAN-yo-el

Emanuel is of Hebrew origin. The meaning of the name Emanuel is "God is with us". A biblical name; borne in the Old Testament to the child whose birth Isaiah foretold. The name was applied to the New Testament, to the coming Messiah. Diminutive: Manny.

Emmanuel

Pronunciation: ee-MAN-yoo-el
Emmanual is of Hebrew origin. The meaning of the name Emmanuel is "God is with us". The Hebrew for of Immanuel. A biblical name; borne in the Old Testament. The name was applied to the New Testament, a name title for the coming Messiah. Diminutive: Manny.

Eric

Pronunciation: AIR-ik
The name Eric is of Old Norse origin. The meaning of Eric is "complete ruler". Old Norse, from ei, 'always', and ric, 'ruler'. The name was introduced to Britain during the 9th century by Scandinavian settlers. The original form is Erik, borne by nine Danish kings. The name was revived in the 19th century. Eric is also used as a nickname for Frederic. Diminutives: Rick, Ricky.

Ernest

Pronunciation: ERN-ist
Ernest is of Old German origin. The meaning of the name Ernest is "seriousness". From the Old German name Ernst, meaning 'earnestness', or 'seriousness.' The Hanoverians introduced the name to Britain during the 18th century. The name became more popular due to Oscar Wilde's play, The Importance of Being Ernest (1899). Diminutives: Ern, Ernie, Erny.

Esmond

Pronunciation: EZ-mund
Esmund is of Old English origin. The meaning of Esmond is "ease of protection". From an Old English name, Eastmund, from east, 'grace', and mund, 'protection'. The name is an adopted surname in modern times, due to the success of Thackeray's History of Henry Esmond (1852).

Ethan

Pronunciation: EE-than
Ethan is of Hebrew origin. The meaning of the name Ethan is "firmness". A biblical name; Ethan the Ezrahite was mentioned in the Old Testament. Known for his wisdom, Solomon was superior in wisdom. Ethan Allen (1738-1789) made the name more popular in America after he played an important role in the American War of Independence.

Eugene

Pronunciation: you-JEEN
The name Eugene is of Greek origin. The meaning of Eugene is "noble aristocrat". From the Old French form of a Greek name, derived from eugenios. 'noble.'

Borne by several saints, two bishops, and four popes. Variations: Eoan, Euan, Ewan, Ewen.

Evan

Pronunciation: EV-an

The name Evan is of Hebrew, Scottish, and Welsh origin. The meaning of Evan is "God is gracious". Anglicisation of Ieuan, Evan is the Welsh form of John. Scotland also uses Evan as an anglicised form of Eoghan. The Hebrew meaning of Evan means "rock."

Evelyn

Pronunciation: EV-e-lyn

Evelyn is of Norman origin. Anglicised form of the Norman French feminine name Aveline. Evelyn is used as both a boy's name, and as a girl's name. The name was adopted as a boy's name in the 17th century. Originally a surname and used as a given name.

Everard

Pronunciation: EV-er-ard

Everard is of Old English and Old German origin. The meaning of the name Everard is "brave, boar". Taken from an Old English name, from eofor, 'boar', and heard, 'strong.' The Norman invaders used an Old German version. The Norman name has been used as a given name since the 19th century.

Ezra

Pronunciation: AIRZ-rah

The name Ezra is of Hebrew origin. The meaning of Ezra is "help". A biblical name; borne by the prophet and author of the fifteenth book of the Bible. Ezra is one of the Old Testament names used by the Puritans.

F

Fabian
Pronunciation: FAY-bee-en
Fabian is of Latin origin. The meaning of the name Fabian is "bean". From the Roman family name Fabius. Borne of 16 saints and a 3rd-century pope. The socialist Fabian Society, founded in 1884, was named after a Roman general who resisted Hannibal's 3rd-century advance on Rome.

Farran
Pronunciation: FA-rran
The name Farran is of Old English and Old French origin. The meaning of Farran is "handsome servant". The name is a variant of the Old English name, Farren.

Felix
Pronunciation: FEEL-iks
The name Felix is of Latin origin. The meaning of Felix is "happy, lucky". From Felicitas, Roman goddess of good fortune and happiness. The name was borne by several saints and three popes. Felix was a popular name for early Christians.

Fergus
Pronunciation: FER-gus
Fergus is of Irish, Gaelic, and Scottish origin. The meaning of the name Fergus is "vigorous man". Irish, anglicised form of the Gaelic name Fearghas, from fear, 'man', and gus, 'vigour'. The name was borne in Irish legend by Fergus mac Roich. Saint Fergus (8th century) was a missionary to Scotland. Diminutive: Fergie

Fenton
Pronunciation: FEN-ton
The name Fenton is of Old English origin. The meaning of Fenton is "marsh settlement". Fenton is also a place name from fenn tûn.

Finbar
Pronunciation: FIN-bar
Finbar is of Gaelic and Irish origin. The meaning of the name Finbar is "white, fair head". Irish, anglicised form of the Gaelic name Fionnbharr, from fionn, 'white, fair', and barr, 'head'. Finbar is a fairy king in Irish mythology. Finbar was a 6th-century bishop of Cork, said to have crossed the Irish Sea on horseback. Diminutives: Finn, Bairre, Barry.

Fingal
Pronunciation: FIN-gal
The name Fingal is of Gaelic and Scottish origin. The meaning of Fingal is "fair, white stranger". Borne in Gaelic legend by the heroic father of Ossian. The name was originally used by the Irish for Norse settlers in Ireland. James Macpherson's poem Fingal (1762).

Finlay
Pronunciation: FIN-lay
Finlay is of Scottish and Gaelic origin. The meaning of the name Finlay is "fair, white warrior". Scottish, anglicised form of the Gaelic name Fionnlagh, from fionn, 'white, fair' and laogh, 'Warrior'.

Finn

Pronunciation: FIN

The name Finn is of Irish, Gaelic, and Old German origin. The meaning of Finn is "white, fair". Irish, anglicised form of Fionn, 'fair, white'. Finn mac Cumhaill is a legendary hero of Irish mythology.

Fletcher

Pronunciation: FLECH-er

Fletcher is of Old French origin. The meaning of the name Fletcher is "arrow maker". The adopted surname is originally an occupational name for an arrow maker. From Old French fleche, 'arrow'. Fletcher Christian was the famous leader of the mutiny on the Bounty in 1789.

Florian

Pronunciation: FLOR-ee-an

The name Florian is of Latin origin. The meaning of Florian is "Flower". Derived from the Latin word flos, 'flower'. From a Roman clan name. Saint Florian was a 3rd-century Roman soldier.

Floyd

Pronunciation: F-lo-yd

The name Floyd is of Welsh origin. The meaning of Floyd is "gray-haired". The adopted Welsh surname is a derivative of Lloyd, from the Welsh llwyd, 'grey'.

Flyn

Pronunciation: FL-yn

Flyn is of Irish and Gaelic origin. The meaning of the name Flyn is "descendant of Flann". The name is a variant of Flynn.

Francesco

Pronunciation: FRAN-ches-CO

Francesco is of Latin origin. The meaning of the name Francesco is "Frenchman". Francesco is a variant of the Latin name, Francis.

Francis

Pronunciation: FRAN-sis

The name Francis is of Latin origin. The meaning of Francis if "Frenchman". Anglicised form of the Italian name Francisco, derived from the Latin Franciscus which means 'French.' France was originally the kingdom of the Franks. The name was assumed by Saint Francis of Assisi (1181-1226), he is known as the gentle giant and associated with nature after preaching to birds. Frances is the feminine form. Diminutives: Frank, Frankie

Franklin

Pronunciation: FRANK-lin

The name Franklin is of Old English origin. The meaning of Franklin is "Freeman". The adopted surname is taken from Old English francoleyn, which means 'a freeman,' specifically a landowner, not of noble birth, typically a prosperous farmer. Diminutives: Frank, Frankie.

Frederick
Pronunciation: FRED-er-ik
The name Frederick is of Old French and
Old German origin. The meaning of
Frederick is "peaceful ruler". The Old
English name Freodhoric was superseded
by the Old German, Frithuric, derived from
frithu, 'peace', and ric, 'ruler'. The
Hanoverians brought the name to Britain in
the 18th century.

G

Gabriel

Pronunciation: GAY-bree-el

The name Gabriel is of Hebrew origin. The meaning of Gabriel is "Hero of God". A biblical name; borne by the name Archangel Gabriel, one of God's chief messengers, and sometimes regarded as the angel of death. In the New Testament, he appeared to Mary and told her that she was to be the mother of Christ. Diminutive: Gabe.

Gareth

Pronunciation: GARE-eth

Gareth is of Welsh origin. The meaning of the name Gareth is "gentle". The name first appeared in Sir Thomas Malory's 15th-century account of the legendary Round Table, Morte D'Arthur. Sir Gareth was well known for his modesty and bravery. Diminutives: Garth, Gary, Garry.

Garfield

Pronunciation: GARF-ield

The name Garfield is of Old English origin. The meaning of Garfield is "spear field". The adopted surname was most likely used as a first name in honour of J. A Garfield (1831-1881), a 20th -century president of the U.S.

Garry

Pronunciation: GAR-ee

The name Garry is of Old English origin. The meaning of Garry is "spear". The name is a diminutive of Gareth. Gary Cooper popularised the name during the 1930's; he had taken the name from his hometown Gary, Indiana.

Gavin

Pronunciation: GAV-en

Gavin is of Welsh origin. The meaning of the name Gavin is "white falcon". The name is a variation of the medieval name Gawain.

Gawain

Pronunciation: GA-wain

The name Gawain is of Welsh and Scottish origin. The meaning of Gawain is "white falcon". The name is a variant of Gavin.

Geoffrey

Pronunciation: JEF-ree

Geoffrey is of Old German origin. The meaning of the name Geoffrey is "peace". The name was introduced to Britain during the Norman Conquest. Geoffrey was a popular name during the medieval era.

George

Pronunciation: JORJ

The name George is of Greek origin. The meaning of George is "farmer". From Greek georgos, meaning 'farmer.' The name was influenced by Old Latin and Old French. Borne by several early saints, including St George, a knight who became the patron saint of England. He achieved legendary status through the medieval story of him slaying a fire-breathing dragon. The legend is a symbolic tale of good triumphing evil, with the dragon being the devil. The name is a royal name, borne by six kings of England.

Gerald

Pronunciation: JARE-ald

The name Gerald is of Old German origin. The meaning of Gerald is "spear ruler". The name was popular during the medieval era and was later revived in the 19th century. Diminutives: Ged, Der, Gerry. Jed, Jerry,

Gerrard

Pronunciation: JARE-ard

The name Gerrard is of Old German origin. The meaning of Gerrard is "spear ruler". The name is a variant of Gerald. The name was popular during the medieval era and later revived during the 19th century. Diminutives: Gerry, Jerry.

Gilbert

Pronunciation: GIL-bert

Gilbert is of Old French origin. The meaning of the name Gilbert is "bright promise". It was a Norman introduction to Britain. Diminutives: Gil, Gilly, Gillie.

Giles

Pronunciation: jiles

The name Giles if of Greek origin. The meaning of Giles is "small goat". The name is an altered version of the Latin name Aegidius, from the Greek name Aigidios. The name refers to the goat skin that ancient shields were made of. St Giles is regarded as the patron saint of cripples, beggars, and blacksmiths. Churches that are dedicated to him are typically located outside of city centers, where cripples were condemned to live.

Glen

Pronunciation: glen

Glen is of Irish and Gaelic origin. The meaning of Glen is "glen". The adopted surname is from Gaelic Gleann, meaning 'valley.' A Glen is a narrow valley between hills. The name is also a place name.

Glyn

Pronunciation: glin

The name Glyn is of Irish and Gaelic origin. The meaning of Glyn is "valley of water". Glyn is a place name. The name is also a variant of Glen. Glyn is used as both a boy's name and as girl's name.

Goldwin

Pronunciation: GOLD-win

The name Goldwin is of Old English origin. The meaning of Goldwin is "golden friend". From the Old English name Goldwine.

Gordon

Pronunciation: GORD-en

Gordon is of Old English and Gaelic origin. The meaning of the name Gordon is "large fortification". An adopted Scottish surname derived from a place-name. The name was first adopted as a first name in honor of Charles Gordon (1833-1885), a British general who was killed at Khartoum.

Graham

Pronunciation: GRAY-em

The name Graham is of Old English origin. The meaning of Graham is "gravel area". The name was derived from the Lincolnshire town of Grantham. The adopted surname was taken to Scotland in the 12th century by Sir William de Graham.

Grant

Pronunciation: GRAN-t

The name Grant is of English and Gaelic origin. The meaning of Grant is "tall, big". An adopted surname derived from French le grand and given to tall men. The name first became popular as a first name in Scotland and America.

Granville

Pronunciation: GRAN-vill

The name Granville of Old French origin. The meaning of Granville is "big town". Originally a place name. Granville is also an adopted French surname, derived from grande ville, which means 'large town.'

Gregory

Pronunciation: GREG-er-ee

Gregory is of Greek origin. The meaning of the name Gregory is "watchful, vigilant". Gregory the great (c. 540-604) was the first of sixteen popes of that name and one of the eleven Doctors of the Western Church. He founded monasteries and remodeled the church liturgy, and developed the Gregorian chants.

Greville

Pronunciation: GREV-vill

The name Greville is of Old French origin. The meaning of Greville is unknown. An adopted surname, from the French name for one from Greville.

Griffin

Pronunciation: GRIF-en

Griffin is of Latin origin. The meaning of Griffin is "hooked nose". Borne in Greek mythology and medieval legend; the Gryphon was a fierce creature with foreparts of an eagle and the hindquarters of a lion.

Guy

Pronunciation: gye

The name Guy is of Old German origin. The meaning of Guy is "wood". From the Old French name Guido, derived from the Old German name Wildo, from witu, meaning 'wood.' Guy was the French name of the early Christian martyr St Vitus. Guy Warwick, a medieval figure of romance and a hero of the Crusades, popularised the name. The name remained popular until it became associated with the leader of the Gunpowder Plot (1605), Guy Fawkes.

Gwyn

Pronunciation: GW-in

The name Gwyn is of Welsh origin. The meaning of Gwyn is "fair, blessed, holy, white". The name is used as both a boy's name, and as a girl's name.

H

Hadrian

Pronunciation: HAY-dree-en

Hadrian is of Latin origin. The meaning of the name Hadrian is "from Hadria". The name is a variation of Adrian. Hadria was a north Italian city.

Haydn

Pronunciation: HAY-den

The name Hayden is of Old English origin. The meaning of Hayden is "hedged valley". The name is conjectured to be a Welsh variant of Aidan.

Hamish

Pronunciation: HA-mish

The name Hamish is of Scottish origin. The meaning of Hamish is "he who supplants". The name is a Scottish form of James.

Harald

Pronunciation: HA-ra-ld

Harald is of Old Norse origin. The meaning of Harald is "army ruler". From Haraldr, an Old Norse form of Harold. The name is a variant of Harold.

Hardy

Pronunciation: HAR-dee

Hardy is of Old German origin. The meaning of Hardy is "bold, brave". Originally from the surname meaning, 'bold'.

Harley

Pronunciation: HAR-lee

The name Harley is of Old English origin. The meaning of Harley is "hare meadow, harewood".

Harold

Pronunciation: HARE-uld

The name Harold is of Old English origin. The meaning of Harold is "army ruler". Old English from here, meaning 'army', and weald, 'power.' The name was influenced by the Old Norse name Haraldr. Diminutive: Harry

Harrison

Pronunciation: HARE-ee-sun

The name Harrison is of Old English origin. The meaning of Harrison is "son of Harry". Harrison is an adopted surname.

Harry

Pronunciation: HARE-ee

The name Harry is of Old German origin. The meaning of Harry is "home leader". The name is a diminutive of Henry or Harold.

Hartley

Pronunciation: HART-lee

Hartley is of Old English origin. The meaning of the name Hartley is "stag meadow". Hartley is an adopted surname from an Old English place name.

Harvey

Pronunciation: HAR-vee

The name Harvey is of Old English and Old French origin. The meaning of Harvey is "eager for battle". The name is a variant of the French name Herve.

Hasan

Pronunciation: HAS-an

The name Hasan if of Arabic origin. The meaning of Hasan is "beautiful, good-looking". The name is a variant of Hassan. Al Hasan was the Prophets grandson, the son of Fatima and Haidar. Hasan and his brother, Husayn are regarded as the rightful successors of Muhammad by the Shiites.

Hector

Pronunciation: HEK-tor

The name Hector is of Greek origin. The meaning of Hector is "to restrain". Greek meaning, 'holding fast'. Borne as the Prince of Troy, Hector was the Trojan hero who was killed by being lashed to his chariot and dragged around the walls of Troy, by Achilles. Diminutives: Heck, Heckie.

Hedley

Pronunciation: HED-lee

The name Hedley is of Old English origin. The meaning of Hedley is "heathered meadow". The name is an adopted surname, derived from an English place name.

Henry

Pronunciation: HEN-ree

Henry is of Old German origin. The meaning of the name Henry is "home ruler". From Old German haim, meaning 'home', and ric, 'ruler.' The name was adopted by the Normans and brought to Britain. The name is borne by eight English Kings. Diminutives: Hal, Hank, Harry, Hen.

Herbert

Pronunciation: HER-bert

The name Herbert is of Old German origin. The meaning of Herbert is "illustrious warrior". The name was brought to Britain by the Normans and died out by the Middle Ages. The name was later revived in the 19th century. Herbert is most notably the family name of the Earls of Pembroke.

Herman

Pronunciation: HER-man

Herman is of Old German origin. The meaning of Herman is "soldier". From the Old German name Hariman, from here, meaning 'army.' The Normans brought the name to Britain, where it died out in the Middle Ages. The name was later revived in the 19th-century. St Herman from the 11th-century wrote hymn "Salve Regina."

Horace

Pronunciation: HOR-ess

The name Horace is of Latin origin. The meaning of Horace is unknown. From the Roman family name Horatius. Borne by Roman lyrical poet, Quintus Horatius Flaccus (65-8BC).

Howard

Pronunciation: HOW-erd

The name Howard is of Old English origin. The meaning of Howard is "noble watchman". An adopted aristocratic and occupational surname. Howard is the family name of the Dukes of Norfolk. The name was used as a given first name during the 19th century.

Howell
Pronunciation: HOWE-ll
The name Howell is of Welsh origin. The meaning of Howell is "eminent, remarkable". Anglicised form of the Welsh name Hywel. Howell is also an adopted surname.

Hugh
Pronunciation: HEW
Hugh is of Old German origin. The meaning of Hugh is "soul, heart, intellect". The name was introduced to Britain by the Normans and became popular during the Middle Ages. St Hugh of Lincoln was a 14th-century bishop of Lincoln.

Humbert
Pronunciation: HUM-bert
The name Humbert is of Old German origin. The meaning of Humbert is "famous warrior". Old French name from Old German hun, meaning 'warrior' and berht, 'bright.' The name was introduced to Britain by the Normans.

Humphrey
Pronunciation: HUM-free
Humphrey is of Old German origin. The meaning of Humphrey is "peaceful warrior". The name was made popular by Hollywood actor, Humphrey Bogart (1899-1957). Diminutive: Humph

I

Iago

Pronunciation: I-ago

The name Iago is of Spanish and Welsh origin. The meaning of Iago is "he who supplants". The name is a variation of the name Jacob. Iago is also a Hebrew variant of the name James. Shakespeare gave the name to his villain in Othello (1604).

Ian

Pronunciation: EE-an

Ian is of Gaelic and Scottish origin. The meaning of the name Ian is "God is gracious". Ian is a Scottish variant of the name John. The name was anglicised to Ian. Iain is the Gaelic spelling.

Ibrahim

Pronunciation: ee-bra-HEEM

The name Ibrahim is of Arabic origin. The meaning of Ibrahim is "father of many". The name is a variant of the Hebrew name Abraham.

Idan

Pronunciation: EE-dan

Idan is of Hebrew origin. The meaning of the name Idan is "era, time".

Idris

Pronunciation: E-dris

The name Idris is of Arabic and Welsh origin. The meaning of Idris is "fiery leader, Prophet". Borne in Welsh legend by a giant magician, astronomer, and prince whose observatory was on Cader Idris. Described in the Koran, the Arabic name was borne by a man described as 'a true man' and 'a prophet', he was also the founder of the

first Shiite dynasty (788-974). The name is used as both a boy's name and, as a girl's name.

Ignatius

Pronunciation: eeg-NAH-see-ers

Ignatius is of Latin origin. The meaning of Ignatius is "fire, burning". From a Roman family name, Egnatius. Borne by several saints, including the Spanish-born Saint Ignatius. Loyola (1491-1556). He founded the Society of Jesus, the Jesuits.

Igor

Pronunciation: EE-gor

The name Igor is of Russian origin. The meaning of Igor is "watchfulness of Ing". The name is a Russian form of the Scandinavian name Ingvarr.

Immanuel

Pronunciation: ih-Man-yoo-el

The name Immanuel is of Hebrew origin. The meaning of Immanuel is "God is with us". The name is a variant of Emmanuel.

Ingram

Pronunciation: IN-gram

The name Ingram is of Old English and Scandinavian origin. The meaning of Ingram is "raven of peace".

Inigo

Pronunciation: I-ni-go

The name Inigo is of Spanish origin. Inigo is a Medieval Spanish variation of Ignatius. St Ignatius Loyola was born Inigo Lopez de Recalde. The name is often associated with the great English architect, Inigo Jones (1573-1652).

Ira
Pronunciation: EYE-rah
Ira is of Hebrew origin. The meaning of the name Ira is "full grown, watchful". From Hebrew, meaning, 'watchful.' A biblical name; borne in the Old Testament, the name of a priest of King David.

Irvine
Pronunciation: EYE-van
Irvine is of Gaelic and Scottish origin. The meaning of the name Irvine is "fresh water". Originally a Scottish surname that was derived from a Celtic river. Irvin is a variation of Irvine or Irving. Irvine is also a place name of a town in Ayrshire.

Isaac
Pronunciation: EYE-zik
The name Isaac is of Hebrew origin. The meaning of Isaac is "laughter". Hebrew, derived from the verb 'to laugh'. A biblical name; borne in the Old Testament he was the only son of Abraham and Sarah. God tested Abraham's faith when Isaac was a young boy, he asked him to sacrifice his son. God relented and provided him with a Ram as a substitute, while Abraham prepared to kill his son. The name was introduced to Britain by the Normans. Izaak is a variation of the name.
Diminutives: Ike, Zak, Zack.

Isaiah
Pronunciation: eye-ZY-ah
Isaiah is of Hebrew origin. The meaning of the name Isaiah is "God is salvation". Hebrew, meaning 'the Lord is generous'. A biblical name; borne by one of the major prophets in the Old Testament. He wrote the book of Isaiah and was best known for foretelling the coming of the Messiah. The name was popular in the 17th century with the Puritans.

Ivan
Pronunciation: EYE-van
The name Ivan is of Hebrew and Russia origin. The meaning of Ivan is "God is gracious". Ivan is the Russin form of the name John. Ivan IV of Russia was famously known as Ivan the Terrible (1533-1584).

Ivor
Pronunciation: EYE-vor
Ivor if of Old Norse and Scandinavian origin. The meaning of the name Ivor is "yew, army". Scandinavian, from Old Norse yr, 'yew' and herr, 'army'. In Welsh, the name is used as a form of Ifor, meaning 'lord.' The name is also used as an anglicised form of the Scottish Gaelic name Lomhar.

J

Jabez
Pronunciation: j(a)-bez
The name Jabez is of Hebrew origin. The meaning of Jabez is "borne in pain". A biblical name; borne in the Old Testament, Jabez is a well-respected man whose prayer to God for blessing was answered (4:9-11).

Jabin
Pronunciation: j(a)-bin
Jabin is of Hebrew origin. The meaning of the name Jabin is "God had built". A biblical name; meaning 'discerner', or 'the wise.'

Jabir
Pronunciation: j(a)bir
The name Jabir is of Arabic origin. The meaning of Jabir is "consolation".

Jacan
Pronunciation: JA-can
The name Jacan is of Hebrew origin. The meaning of Jacan is "trouble". A biblical name; he is mentioned as a family leader of the tribe of Gad (5:13).

Jace
Pronunciation: jayce
Jace is of English origin. The meaning of the name Jayce is "the Lord is my salvation". The name is a short form of the Hebrew name Jason.

Jachin
Pronunciation: j(a)-chin
The name Jachin is of Hebrew origin. The meaning of Jachin is "he establishes". A biblical name; Jachin and Boaz were the names given by their craftsman to two large cast bronze pillars, which stood on either side of the entrance to the Temple in Jerusalem. Built by King Solomon according to God's instructions.

Jacinto
Pronunciation: ha-CEEN-toh
Jacinto is of Spanish and Greek origin. The meaning of Jacinto is unknown. Jacinto is a masculine form of the Greek flower name, Hyacinth.

Jack
Pronunciation: jak
Jack is of Old English origin. The meaning of the name Jack is "God is gracious". Jack is a diminutive of John. The name was popular during the Middle Ages and has recently undergone a new surge in popularity.

Jacob
Pronunciation: JAY-kub
The name Jacob is of Hebrew origin. The meaning of Jacob is "he who supplants". An anglicised form of the Hebrew name Yaakov. A biblical name; borne by the greatest patriarch of the Old Testament, the son of Isaac and Rebekah. He was the father of the twelve tribes of Israel. After wrestling with an angel, he was given the name Israel and became the ancestor of the nation of Israel.

Jamil
Pronunciation: JA-mil

The name Jamil if of Arabic origin. The meaning of Jamil is "handsome, graceful". The name is a variant of Jamal.

James

Pronunciation: jayms

The name James is of Hebrew origin. The meaning of James is "he who supplants". The name is a variation of Jacob, derived from the Latin form, Jacomus. A biblical name; borne in the New Testament by one of the twelve apostles of Jesus. He was a relative of Jesus, possibly a brother or a cousin. The name spread to Britain and became popular during the 13th century. The name became associated with the royal house Stuart. Diminutives: Jamie, Jem, Jim, Jimmy, Jemmy.

Jared

Pronunciation: JARE-ed

The name Jared is of Hebrew origin. The meaning Jared is "descending, rose". A biblical name; borne in the Old Testament by the father of Enoch. Jared was a pre-Flood ancestor of Jesus. The Puritan adoption underwent a revival in the 1960's. This was possibly due to the TV Western Big Valley (1965-1969), with its character Jarrod.

Jason

Pronunciation: JAY-sun

The name Jason is of Greek and Hebrew origin. The meaning of Jason is "healer; the Lord is salvation". The name is a variant of Joshua. A biblical name; borne by an early Christian associate of Paul. Jason is an anglicised form of a Greek name, borne in Greek mythology. Jason was the leader of Argonauts who sailed his ship to Argos in search of the Golden Fleece.

Jasper

Pronunciation: JAS-per

Jasper is of Greek origin. The meaning of the name Jasper is "treasure holder". English form of the French name, Gasper, and the German name, Caspar. In medieval tradition, the name was given to one of the three Magi. Jasper is also the name of a gemstone.

Jeremiah

Pronunciation: jare-ah-MYE-ah

The name Jeremiah is of Hebrew origin. The meaning of Jeremiah is "appointed by God". A biblical name; borne by one of the major 7th century BC Hebrew Prophets. The scholar was the author of the Book of Lamentations and the Book of Jeremiah. The name was popular among the Puritans. Diminutive: Jerry.

Jerome

Pronunciation: jer-OME

The name Jerome is of Greek origin. The meaning of Jerome is "sacred name". From Greek, meaning 'holy name.' Saint Jeroma (c. 342-420), was a biblical scholar who translated the Vulgate Bible into Latin, for the Western Church. He is often portrayed with a lion beside him, while he is writing or studying in cardinal's dress. His feast day is 30th September. Diminutive: Jerry.

Jesse

Pronunciation: JESS-ee

Jesse is of Hebrew origin. The meaning of the name Jesse is "God exists". A biblical name; borne in the Old Testament by the shepherd father of King David, from whom the ancestry of Christ can be traced. Jesse was adopted by the Puritans. The name was revived in the 20th century.

Jethro

Pronunciation: JETH-roh

The name Jethro is of Hebrew origin. The meaning of Jethro is "pre-eminence, eminent". A biblical name; borne in the Old Testament by Moses's father in law. The name was common among Puritans.

Jocelyn

Pronunciation: JOS-e-lyn

The name Jocelyn is of Old German origin. The meaning of Jocelyn is "one of the Goths". The name was introduced to Britain by the Normans. Jocelyn is used as both a boy's name, and as a girl's name. Diminutive: Joss.

Joel

Pronunciation: JOH-ul

The name Joel is of Hebrew origin. The meaning of Joel is "Jehovah is the Lord". A biblical name: borne by a prophet of the 8th century BC, he was also the author of the Old Testament Book of Joel.

John

Pronunciation: JO-hn

John is of Hebrew origin. The meaning of the name John is "God is gracious". A biblical name; borne by several figures, including the longest-lived of the twelve apostles. St John the Baptist, who was the relative and forerunner of Christ. He was sent 'to prepare the way of the Lord' and baptized Christ in the Jordan River. The name is possibly the most popular name in history, borne by numerous saints, popes, and kings. Diminutives: Hank, Jack, Jock, Johnnie, Johnny.

Johnathan

Pronunciation: JOHN-a-thun

The name Johnathan is of Hebrew origin. The meaning of Johnathan is "gift of God". The name is a variant of Jonathan. Diminutives: Johnnie, Johnny, John, Jon.

Jonathan

Pronunciation: JAHN-a-thun

Jonathan is of Hebrew origin. The meaning of the name Jonathan is "gift of God; God has given". A biblical name; borne in the Old Testament by the son of King Saul, Jonathan was renowned for his manliness and generosity. He was also a great friend of King David; he later saved his life from Saul. Jonathan was eventually killed in battle. The name was adopted by the Puritans. Diminutives: Johnnie, Johnny, Jon.

Jordan

Pronunciation: JOR-dan

Jordan is of Hebrew origin. The meaning of the name Jordan is "down-flowing". From the name of the river in the Middle East where Christ was baptized by John the Baptist. The name has been used as a first name since the Crusades. The name underwent a popular revival in the 1980's. Jordan is used as both a boy's name, and as a girl's name.

Joseph

Pronunciation: JOH-sef

The name Joseph is of Hebrew origin. The meaning of Joseph is "Jehovah increases, God will add". A biblical name; borne by three major figures. The son of Jacob and Rachel, Joseph was sold into slavery by his jealous brothers. He later became an important advisor to the Pharaoh and supreme power in Egypt. St Joseph the husband of Virgin Mary and the earthly father of Jesus. He is the patron saint of carpenters, and his feast day is 19th March. St Joseph of Arimathea was a rich Jew who would not declare his faith publicly. He was the one who brought Christ down from the cross and buried him in a private tomb. Diminutives: Jo, Joe.

Joshua

Pronunciation: JOSH-yoo-ah

Joshua is of Hebrew origin. The meaning of the name Joshua is "God is salvation". A biblical name; Joshua was an attendant to Moses and later succeeded him as the leader of the Israelites. Joshua is also known for leading the defeat of the city of Jericho by the blowing of trumpets. Diminutive: Josh.

Jude

Pronunciation: JU-de

The name Jude is of Greek origin. The meaning of Jude is "praised". The name is a variation of Judas. A biblical name; the Apostle St Jude was the author of the New Testament epistle of Jude. He is regarded as the patron saint of hopeless causes. Thomas Hardy popularised the name during the 19th century with his novel, Jude the Obscure (1895).

Julian

Pronunciation: JOO-lee-en

The name Julian is of Greek origin. The meaning of Julian is "Jove's child". From the Roman family name Julius. Julian is borne by several saints. The name was brought to Britain during the Middle Ages.

Julius

Pronunciation: JU-li-us

Julius is of Greek origin. The meaning of the name Julius is "Jove's child". A Roman family name of several of the most powerful Roman emperors, including Emperor Gaius Julius Caesar.

Justin

Pronunciation: JUS-tin

The name Justin is of Latin origin. The meaning of Justin is "fair, just". From the Latin name Justinius, derived from justus, meaning 'just.' Borne by four saints, St Justin (2nd century) was a Greek philosopher who wrote of the moral values of Christianity. The name was also borne by Byzantine emperors. The name Justin was revived in the 20th century.

K

Kacey

Pronunciation: KAY-see

The name Kacey is a variant of Casey. Kacey is used as both a boy's name, and as a girl's name

Kade

Pronunciation: kayd

Kade if of Scottish origin. The meaning of the name Kade is "from the wetlands". The name is also a variant of Cade.

Kaden

Pronunciation: KAYD-en

The name Kaden is of Arabic origin. The meaning of Kaden is "Companion". Kaden is also an Old German place name.

Kamal

Pronunciation: KA-mal

Kamal is of Arabic origin. The meaning of Kamal is "perfection". The name is also found in India, where its origin is from Sanskrit.

Kane

Pronunciation: KAYN

The name Kane is of Gaelic and Irish origin. The meaning of Kane is "battle". Anglicised form of the Irish Gaelic name Cathán, derived from cath, 'battle'.

Kareem

Pronunciation: kah-REEM

Kareem is of Arabic origin. The meaning of the name Kareem is "generous, noble".

Karl

Pronunciation: karl

The name Karl is of Old German origin. The meaning of Karl is "free man". Karl is the German form of Charles.

Kavanagh

Pronunciation: KAV-a-nagh

The name Kavanagh is of Irish and Gaelic origin. The meaning of Kavanagh is "follower of Kevin". Originally an Irish surname.

Kay

Pronunciation: KAY

The name Kay is of Latin and Old Welsh origin. The meaning of Kay is "happy". An ancient name borne in the legend by a knight of the Round Table. Kay is used as both a boy's name, and as a girl's name.

Keanu

Pronunciation: kee-AH-noo

Keanu is of Hawaiian origin. The meaning of the name Keanu is "cool breeze from the mountains".

Keegan

Pronunciation: KEE-gan

The name Keegan is of Irish and Gaelic origin. The meaning of Keegan is "little fiery one".

Keir

Pronunciation: KEE-er

The name Keir is of Gaelic origin. The meaning of Keir is "dusky, dark haired". The name may have been adopted in honor of the first Labour MP, James Keir Hardie (1856-1915). Actor Keir Dullea also made the name popular during the 1970's.

Kelvin

Pronunciation: KEL-vin

The name Kelvin is of English origin. The meaning of Kelvin is "friend of ships". Kelvin is also a place name referring to a Scottish river.

Kendall

Pronunciation: KEN-dal

The name Kendall is of Old English origin. The meaning of the name Kendall is "the Kent River Valley". An adopted surname, from a Cumbrian place name, Kendal. The name is used as both a boy's name, and as a girl's name. Kendal has been used as a given name since the 19th century.

Kendrick

Pronunciation: KEN-drik

Kendrick if of Welsh origin. The meaning of the name Kendrick is "greatest champion". An adopted Welsh surname, derived from an early first name, Cywrig. The name is also possibly from Old Welsh cyne, 'royal', and ric, 'ruler'.

Kenneth

Pronunciation: KEN-eth

Kenneth is of Irish and Gaelic origin. The meaning of the name Kenneth is "handsome". Anglicisation of the Gaelic name Cainnech, which means 'handsome.' Diminutives: Ken, Kenny.

Kent

Pronunciation: KENT

Kent is of Old English origin. The meaning of the name Kent is "edge". The adopted surname is also a place name derived from the English county.

Kenton

Pronunciation: KENT-on

The name Kenton is of Old English origin. The meaning of Kenton is "the royal settlement". An adopted surname and English place name.

Kester

Pronunciation: KES-ter

Kester is of Greek and Gaelic origin. The meaning of the name Kester is "bearing Christ". Kester is a Medieval diminutive of Christopher.

Kevin

Pronunciation: KEV-in

The name Kevin is of Irish and Gaelic origin. The meaning of Kevin is "handsome beloved". Anglicisation of the Irish Gaelic name Caoimnin, from caomh, 'handsome'. Borne by an Irish hermit saint of the 7th century, he was the patron saint of Dublin. The name was rarely used outside of Ireland until the 20th century when it became hugely popular. Diminutive: Kev.

Kieran

Pronunciation: KEER-en

Kieran is of Irish and Gaelic origin. The meaning of the name Kieran is "black". Anglicisation of the Irish Gaelic name Ciaran, which means 'dark.' Borne by two Celtic saints of the 5th and 6th century. The name was revived and became popular during the 20th century.

Kim
Pronunciation: KIM
The name Kim is of English origin. The meaning of Kim is "gold". Originally a diminutive of Kimball or Kimberley. The name is used as both a boy's name, and as a girl's name.

Kingsley
Pronunciation: KINGS-lee
The name Kingsley is of Old English origin. The meaning of Kingsley is "king's meadow". The adopted surname is also a place name, from the Old English name Cyningesleah, which means 'king's wood.' Writer Charles Kingsley (1817-1875) made the name more popular in the 19th century.

Kingston
Pronunciation: KING-ston
The name Kingston is of Old English origin. The meaning of Kingston is "King's settlement". Kingston is also a place name.

Konrad
Pronunciation: KAHN-rad
The name Konrad is of Polish and German origin. The meaning of Konrad is "bold advisor". The name is a variant of the Old German name Conrad. From German rad 'counsel' and conja, meaning 'bold.'

Kumar
Pronunciation: KU-mar
The name Kumar is of Hindi and Sanskrit origin. The meaning of Kumar is "male child".

Kurt
Pronunciation: KURT
Kurt is of German origin. The meaning of the name Kurt is "courageous advice". The name is a variant of the Old German name Conrad.

Kyle
Pronunciation: KYL
The name Kyle is of Gaelic origin. The meaning of Kyle is "straight". An adopted Scottish place name, from the Scottish term kyle, which means 'straight', or 'channel.' Derived from the Gaelic caol, 'narrow'. Kyle is the name of the central district of Ayrshire in western Strathclyde.

L

Lachlan

Pronunciation: LOCH-lan

The name Lachlan is of Irish and Gaelic origin. The meaning of Lachlan is "from the land of lakes". From the Scottish name Lachlann, the Gaelic word for Norway. Diminutive: Lockie.

Lambert

Pronunciation: LAMB-bert

Lambert is of Scandinavian origin. The meaning of the name Lambert is "land brilliant". Old German from landa. St Lambert popularised the name in medieval Belgium and Netherlands. He was a 7th-century bishop of Maastricht. The name spread to Britain in the Middle Ages.

Lance

Pronunciation: LANCE

The name Lance is of French origin. The meaning of Lance is "land". French from the Old German name Lanzo. Diminutives: Lancelot, Launcelot.

Lancelot

Pronunciation: LANS-e-lot

The name Lancelot is of Old French origin. The meaning of Lancelot is "servant". Borne in Arthurian legend by the most famous knight of the Round Table, Lancelot du Lac. His seduction of Queen Guinevere started a war that resulted in the destruction of the Round Table, and the death of King Author.

Laurence

Pronunciation: LAUR-ence

The name Laurence is of French origin. The meaning of Laurence is "from Laurentium", an ancient Italian town of olive groves. Laurence is a variant of the Latin name Lawrence. Borne by a 3rd-century deacon of Roman, he was martyred in 258 by being roasted on a gridiron. He is considered the patron saint of curriers and his feast day is 10th August. Diminutives: Lanty, Larry, Laurie, Lawri.

Lee

Pronunciation: LEE

Lee is of Old English origin. The meaning of the name Lee is "wood, meadow, clearing". An adopted surname and place name. Lee was first used as a first name in the 19th century, probably in honor of the Confederate general Robert E. Lee (1807-1870). The name is used as both a boy's name and as a girl's name.

Leighton

Pronunciation: LAY-ton

The name Leighton is of Old English origin. The meaning of Leighton is "meadow settlement". The adopted surname was derived from the place name, from Old England leac. Leighton has been used as a first name since the 19th century.

Lennox

Pronunciation: LEN-iks

The name Lennox is of Gaelic and Scottish origin. The meaning of Lennox is "with many elm trees". An adopted Scottish surname, from the Levenach. The name also appears in Shakespeare's Macbeth (1606).

Leo

Pronunciation: LEE-oh

The name Leo is of Latin origin. The meaning of the name Leo is "Lion". From Latin leo. The name was popular in Roman times. Leo is the fifth sign of the zodiac. The name was borne by thirteen popes, including Leo the Great (5th century) and four saints.

Leon

Pronunciation: LEE-ahn

Leon is of Greek origin. The meaning of the name Leon is "Lion". Lion is a variant of Leo.

Leonard

Pronunciation: LEN-ard

The name Leonard is of Old German origin. The meaning of Leonard is "lion strength". From the Old German name Leonhard. The name was popularised in the 6th century by St Leonard; he was a Frank at the court of Clovis. He is the patron saint of prisoners, and his feast day is 6th November. Diminutives: Len, Lennie, Lenny, Leo.

Leslie

Pronunciation: LEZ-lee

The name Leslie is of Gaelic and Scottish origin. The meaning of Leslie is "Holly Garden". An adopted Scottish surname derived from the place name Lesslyn. It was used as a first name in the 19th century. Diminutive: Les.

Lester

Pronunciation: LES-ter

The name Lester is of Old English origin. The meaning of Lester is "from Leicester". The adopted surname was adopted in the 19th century.

Lewis

Pronunciation: LOO-iss

The name Lewis is of Old German origin. The meaning of Lewis is "famous warrior". An anglicised form of the name Louis.

Liam

Pronunciation: LEE-am

Liam is of Old German origin. The meaning of the name Liam is "determined protector". The name is originally a diminutive of Uilliam, an Irish variation of William. The name became popular in its own right.

Lincoln

Pronunciation: LINK-en

The name Lincoln is of Old English origin. The meaning of Lincoln is "lake colony". An adopted surname and English place name originally used to indicate 'the Roman colony at the lake'. Abraham Lincoln (1809-1865) popularised the name as a first name. He was the 16th president of the US whose presidency won the Civil War and abolished slavery.

Lindsay

Pronunciation: LIN-d-say

Lindsay is of Old English origin. The meaning of the name Lindsay is "Lincoln's marsh". Sir Walter de Lindesay brought the name to Scotland from Lindsey, Lincolnshire. The name is used as both a boy's name and as a girl's name.

Linford
Pronunciation: LIN-ford
The name Linford is of Old English origin. The meaning of Linford is "linden tree ford". An adopted surname and English place name.

Linus
Pronunciation: LYE-nus
The name Linus is of Greek origin. The meaning of Linus is "flax". The name is a Latin form of the Greek name Linos. A biblical name; borne by a Christian companion to Paul in Rome. In Greek mythology, Linus is the name of Hercules's music tutor.

Lionel
Pronunciation: LYE-a-nel
The name Lionel is of Latin origin. The meaning of Lionel is "Lion". The name is originally a medieval diminutive of Leon. The name was borne by a knight of King Author's Round Table.

Llewellyn, Llewelyn
Pronunciation: loo-ELL-en
The name Llewellyn is of Welsh origin. The meaning of Llewellyn is "like a lion, leader". Borne by two 13th-century Welsh

princes, Llewelyn ap Iorwerth and Llywelyn ap Gruffydd.

Lloyd
Pronunciation: loyd
The name Lloyd is of Welsh origin. The meaning of Lloyd is "gray haired". An anglicised form of the Welsh name Llwyd.

Louis
Pronunciation: LOO-iss
The name Louis is of French and Old German origin. The meaning of Louis is "famous warrior". From the Old German name Chlodovech. The name was borne by nineteen kings of France and numerous saints. Diminutive: Lou.

Lucas
Pronunciation: LOO-kas
Lucas is of Greek origin. The meaning of the name Lucas is "man of Lucania", in southern Italy. The name is a variation of Loukas. The name was introduced to Britain in the 12th century.

Lucian
Pronunciation: LOO-shun
The name Lucian is of Latin origin. The meaning of Lucian is "light". From the Roman clan name Lucianus. St Lucian of Antioch was a 4th-century scholar.

Lucius
Pronunciation: LOU-cius

The name Lucius is of Latin origin. The meaning of Lucius is "light". From Latin lux. Lucius was a popular name in Ancient Rome. The name was borne by three popes.

Luke
Pronunciation: LOO-k
The name Luke is of Greek origin. The meaning of Luke is "man of Lucania", a region in southern Italy. A biblical name; St Luke the Evangelist, apparently wrote the third gospel and the Acts of the Apostles. He is a patron saint of doctors and artists and is described in the Bible as a physician (Colossians 4:14).

Lyall
Pronunciation: LYE-al
The name Lyall is of Old Norse origin. The meaning of Lyall is "Wolf". From an Old Norse name, Liulfr.

Lyle
Pronunciation: LYE-el
The name Lyle is of Old French origin. The meaning of Lyle is "the island". An adopted Scottish surname, from Old French de lisle, which means 'of the island.'

Lyndon
Pronunciation: LIN-dan
The name Lyndon is of Old English origin. The meaning of Lyndon is "linden tree hill". Lyndon is an adopted surname and place name. The name became popular in America after Lyndon Baines Johnson (1908-1978), who was the 36th president.

M

Mackenzie

Pronunciation: ma-KEN-zee
The name Mackenzie if of Gaelic and Irish origin. The meaning of Mackenzie is "son of the wise ruler". An adopted Scottish surname, from Gaelic Mac Coinnich. Mackenzie is used as both a boy's name, and as a girl's name.

Magnus

Pronunciation: MAG-ness
The name Magnus is of Latin origin. The meaning of Magnus is "great". The name was adopted by St Olaf of Norway, an admirer of Charlemagne. The name is borne by several Norwegian Kings and several Scandinavian saints. The name was introduced from Scandinavia to Scotland by one of the Saints, who visited the Scottish islands of Orkney and Shetland.

Malachi

Pronunciation: MAL-a-kye
Malachi is of Hebrew origin. The meaning of the name Malachi is "messenger of God". A biblical name; borne by the author of the last book of the Old Testament, and a prophet. His prophesies focus mainly on the coming of Judgment Day. The name is believed to have come from the text itself: 'Behold, I will send my messenger, and he shall prepare the way before me' (Malachi 3:1).

Malachy

Pronunciation: MAL-a-key
The name Malachy is of Hebrew origin. The meaning of Malachy is "messenger of God". The name is a variant of Malachi.

The name was first adopted in reference to an early Irish King, Maoileachlainn. The name was popularised in the 12th century by St Malachy (1095-1148), he was a bishop of Armagh.

Malcolm

Pronunciation: MAL-cum
Malcolm is of Gaelic and Scottish origin. The meaning of the name Malcolm is "devotee of Saint Columba". Anglicised from the Gaelic name Mael Coluim. The name was borne by four medieval Scottish kings. Malcolm is also the name of the prince of Scotland who became King of Scotland after Macbeth murdered his father. Shakespeare immortalised the true story in his play, Macbeth (1606).

Mallory

Pronunciation: MALL-or-ee
The name Mallory is of Old French origin. The meaning of Mallory is "unfortunate". The name is used as both a boy's name and as a girl's name.

Manfred

Pronunciation: MAN-fred
The name Manfred is of Old German origin. The meaning of Manfred is "man of peace". From Old German man, meaning 'man', and fred, 'peace.' The name was introduced to Britain by the Normans and fell out of use after the Middle Ages. Manfred was later revived in the 19th century. Lord Byron used the name for his epic poem Manfred (1817).

Manley

Pronunciation: MAN-lee

The name Manley is of Old English origin. The meaning of Manley is "shared land, wood". Manley is also a place name.

Marius

Pronunciation: MAR-ee-us

Marius is of Latin origin. The meaning of the name Marius is "dedicated to Mars". The name is an adaptation of the Roman family name Marius, from Mars, Roman god of war. The name is also a variant of Mario.

Mark

Pronunciation: MAR-k

The name Mark is of Latin origin. The meaning of Mark is "dedicated to Mars". The name is an anglicised form of the Latin name, Marcus. A biblical name; borne in the New Testament by St Mark, author of the second Gospel who died in c. 68. His feast day is 25th April.

Marshall

Pronunciation: MAR-shal

The name Marshal is of Old French origin. The meaning of Marshall is "caretaker of horses". An adopted surname, originally derived from a Norman French occupational name for a groom, mareshcal. Marshall is also a law enforcement title and a military title. The name has been used as a first name since the early 19th century.

Martin

Pronunciation: MART-en

Martin is of Latin origin. The meaning of the name Martin is "dedicated to Mars". Martin is an anglicised form of the Latin name Martinus. The name originates with the Roman war god, Mars. St Martin of Tours (c. 316-97) popularised the name throughout medieval Europe. He was converted to Christianity while a soldier in Rome and later became bishop of Tours. He is best known for cutting his cloak in two and sharing it with a beggar. His feast day is 11th November.   Civil rights activist Martin Luther King popularised the name in the 20th century.

Matthew

Pronunciation: MATH-yoo

The name Matthew is of Hebrew origin. The meaning of Matthew is "gift of God". A biblical name; borne in the New Testament by one of Christ's twelve apostles. Also known as Levi, he wrote the first Gospel account of the life of Jesus. His feast day is 21st September. Matthew is the form of the Hebrew name, Mattathia. The name was introduced to Britain by the Norman's. Diminutives: Mat, Matt, Mattie.

Matthias

Pronunciation: ma-THYE-us

The name Mattias is of Greek, Hebrew, and German origin. The meaning of Mattias is "gift of God". New Testament Greek form of the Hebrew name Mattathia. A biblical name; borne in the New Testament by the disciple who was selected to replace Judas as an Apostle, 'the thirteenth apostle' (Acts 1:23-26).

Maurice

Pronunciation: maw-REESE
Maurice is of Latin origin. The meaning of the name Maurice is "Moorish".
From the Latin name Mauricius. Borne by a 3rd-century saint who was martyred in Switzerland. The Roman name was introduced to Britain by the Normans.

Maxim

Pronunciation: MAX-im
Maxim is of Latin origin. The meaning of the name Maxim is "greatest". The name is a variation of Maximus. The name was used by Daphne du Maurier in his novel, Rebecca (1940). Maxim is also the name of three Roman emperors and several early saints.

Maximilian

Pronunciation: MAX-i-mi-lian
The name Maximilian is of Latin origin. The meaning of Maximilian is "greatest". From the Latin name Maximilianus. Borne by a 3rd-century martyr. The name of three Roman emperors and several early saints.

Maxwell

Pronunciation: MAKS-wel
The name Maxwell is of Old English origin. The meaning of Maxwell is "Mack's stream". An adopted Scottish surname and place name. The name has been used in

Scotland since the mid-19th century

Maynard

Pronunciation: MAY-nerd
The name Maynard is of Old German origin. The meaning of Maynard is "brave, strength". Maynard is an adopted surname, originally from Norman French magin, meaning 'strength.' The name was introduced to Britain by the Normans.

Melville

Pronunciation: MEL-ville
The name Melville is of Old French origin. The meaning of Melville is "bad settlement". Originally a Norman French baronial name derived from Malleville. The surname was adopted by those fleeing to Scotland from a poor settlement in northern France. Herman Melville (author of Moby Dick), popularised the name during the 19th century. Diminutive: Mel.

Melvin

Pronunciation: MEL-vin
The name Melvin in of uncertain origins. Possibly a variation of Melville or a masculine form of Malvina. Diminutive: Mel.

Merlin

Pronunciation: MER-lin
Merlin is of Welsh origin. The meaning of the name Melvin is "sea fortress". From the Latinate form, Merlinus, of the Old Welsh name Myrddin. Borne in Arthurian legend by magician Merlin Ambrosius. The name is used as both a boy's name, and as a girl's

name.

Merton

Pronunciation: MERT-on

Merton is of Old English origin. The meaning of the name Merton is "town by the lake". Merton is an adopted surname and English place name, from Old English mere, meaning 'lake', and tun, 'settlement.'

Michael

Pronunciation: MYE-kal

The name Michael is of Hebrew origin. The meaning of Michael is "who is like God?" A biblical name; borne by St Michael the Archangel who defeated the dragon. He was the leader of the seven archangels and leader of the celestial armies. Angels, Michael and Gabriel, are given personal names in the canonical Bible. Several saints, Emperors, and Kings have borne the name. Michael has been popular in the English-speaking world since the Middle Ages. Diminutives: Mick, Mickey, Micky, Mike, Mikey, Mischa, Misha, Mitch.

Miles

Pronunciation: myls

The name Miles if of Latin origin. The meaning of Miles is "soldier". Derived from Latin miles, meaning 'solider,' owing to the military association of St Michael the Archangel.

Montgomery

Pronunciation: mon-GOH-mer-ree

The name Montgomery is of Old French origin. The meaning of Montgomery is "mountain of the powerful one". Montgomery is an adopted surname, and originally a Norman baronial name and place name, from Calvados. The Welsh county of Montgomeryshire was named after a Norman settler. Montgomery is the surname of English and Scottish earls.

Mordecai

Pronunciation: MOR-de-cai

Mordecai is of Hebrew origin. The meaning of the name Mordecai is "little man, follower of Marduk (a god of the Babylonians)". A biblical name; borne in the Old Testament by a cousin and guardian of Esther. Mordecai warned Esther of Haman's plans to massacre all Jews (Esther 4-7). The name was popular in the 17th and 18th century.

Morley

Pronunciation: MOOR-lee

The name Morley is of Old English origin. The meaning of Morley is "meadow on the moor". An adopted surname and English place name.

Mortimer

Pronunciation: MORT-im-er

Mortimer is of Old French origin. The meaning of the name Mortimer is "dead sea". Mortimer is an adopted aristocratic surname, itself derived from a Norman baronial name and place name, Mortimer in Normandy. The name has been used as a first name since the 19th century.

Morton
Pronunciation: MORT-on
The name Morton is of Old English origin. The meaning of Morton is "moor town, settlement on the moor'. An adopted surname and English place name. Morton has been used as a first name since the 19th century.

Moses
Pronunciation: MOH-ziz
Moses is of Hebrew and possibly Egyptian origin. The meaning of Moses is "saviour". Anglicised form of the Hebrew name Moshe. A biblical name; borne by the Hebrew baby who was found floating on the River Nile and adopted by an Egyptian Pharaoh's daughter. Moses was a patriarch who led the Israelites out of Egypt for the Promised Land. The name was popular in medieval Britain and was later revived by the Puritans after the Reformation.

Mostyn
Pronunciation: MOS-tyn
The name Mostyn is of Welsh origin. The meaning of Mostyn is "mossy settlement". An adopted Welsh surname and place name in Clywd, North Wales.

Muhammad
Pronunciation: mo-HAM-med
The name Muhammad is of Arabic origin. The meaning of Muhammad is "praiseworthy". Borne by the Prophet and founder of Islam, Abu al-Qasim Muhammad. He was borne at Mecca in c.570 and died in Medina in 632. Mohammad is one of the most popular Islamic boy's names.

Murray
Pronunciation: MUR-ee
The name Murray is of Gaelic origin. The meaning of Murray is "sea". Murray is an adopted Scottish surname, from Scottish Gaelic muir. Murray is the surname of an ancient Scottish clan. The name was adopted as a first name in the 19th century.

Myron
Pronunciation: MYE-an
The name Myron is of Greek origin. The meaning of Myron is "myrrh, fragrant oil". Borne by a Greek sculptor of the 5th century BC, he was renowned for his realistic statues of athletes, animals, and gods.

N

Naim

Pronunciation: NA-im

The name Naim is of Arabic origin. The meaning of Naim is "comfortable, tranquil". Variations: Naeem.

Nairn

Pronunciation: NA-ir-n

The name Nairn is of Scottish and Gaelic origin. The meaning of Nairn is "river with alder trees". Celtic dweller by the alder tree. Nairn is also a place name.

Nathan

Pronunciation: NAY-than

Nathan is of Hebrew origin. The meaning of the name Nathan is "God has given". Hebrew, meaning 'gift.' A biblical name: borne in the Old Testament, Nathan was God's prophet who advised King David to build the temple during the reigns of David and Solomon.

Nathaniel

Pronunciation: na-THAN-yel

The name Nathaniel is of Hebrew origin. The meaning of Nathaniel is "God has given". Hebrew, meaning 'gift of God.' A biblical name; borne in the New Testament by one of Christ's twelve Apostles. He was also known as Bartholomew. Shakespeare used the name Nathaniel in Love's Labour's Lost (1594). Diminutives: Nat, Nath, Nathan.

Ned

Pronunciation: ned

The name Ned is of English origin. The meaning of Ned is "wealthy guard". Ned is used as a nickname for Edward.

Neil

Pronunciation: neel

Neil is of Irish and Gaelic origin. The meaning of Neil is "Champion". The name is a Scottish variation of Niall which dates back to the Middle Ages.

Nelson

Pronunciation: NEL-sun

The name Nelson is of Irish and Gaelic origin. The meaning of Nelson is unknown. The adopted surname was first used as a first name in the 19th century. Naval hero of Trafalgar, Admiral Lord Horatio Nelson (1758-1805) popularised the name.

Neville

Pronunciation: NEV-il

The name Neville is of Old French origin. The meaning of Neville is "new village". Neville is an adopted aristocratic surname and Old French place name. From Old French, neuve, meaning 'new', and ville, 'town.' It was introduced to Britain during the Norman Conquest.

Niall

Pronunciation: NYE-al

Niall is of Irish and Gaelic origin. The meaning of Niall is "Champion". Borne by a 5th-century Irish king, Niall of the Nine Hostages.

Nicholas

Pronunciation: NIK-oh-lus

Nicholas is of Greek origin. The meaning of the name Nicholas is "people of victory".

Anglicised from the Greek name Nikolaos, from nike, meaning 'victory', and laos, 'people.' A biblical name: borne by one of seven qualified men in the first-century Christian congregation. The name is also borne by a 4th-century bishop of Myra who is now considered patron saint of Greece and Russia, as well as children, scholars, sailors and pawnbrokers. St Nicholas, in his Dutch incarnation of Santa Claus is well known throughout the Christian world for bringing Christmas presents.

Nigel
Pronunciation: NYE-jel
The name Nigel if of Gaelic and Irish origin. The meaning of Nigel is "Champion". The name was revived in the 19th century, during the craze for medieval names.

Noel
Pronunciation: NOH-el
Noel is of French origin. The meaning of the name Noel is "Christmas". An Old French, form noel, which was derived from the Latin dies natalis, meaning birthday. Referring directly to the birthday of Christ. The name is used as both a boy's name, and as a girl's name.

Norman
Pronunciation: NOR-mahn
The name Norman is of Old German origin. The meaning of Norman is "northerner". Derived from Old German nord, 'north', and man, 'man'. The name was already in use in Britain before the Norman Conquest. However, it was then reinforced and used to describe the Norman invaders and their descendants. The name was revived in the 19th century. Diminutive: Norm.

111

Odysseus

Pronunciation: OD-ys-seus

Odysseus is of Greek origin. The meaning of the name Odysseus is "angry man". Original Greek form of the hero of Homer's epic, the Odyssey.

Olaf

Pronunciation: OH-loff

The name Olaf is of Old Norse origin. The meaning of Olaf is "ancestor's relic". From the Old Norse name Anleifr, meaning 'relic of his ancestor's.' A royal name in Norway. It was borne by several Scandinavian kings, including St Olaf, patron saint of Norway.

Oliver

Pronunciation: AH-lih-ver

Oliver is of Latin origin. The meaning of the name Oliver is "olive tree". The name may be a variation of Olaf. The name fell from favor after the death of Oliver Cromwell (1599-1658) but became popular again in the 19th century. Possibly due to the influence of Charles Dickens's novel Oliver Twist (1838). Diminutives: Noll, Ol, Ollie,

Omar

Pronunciation: OH-mar

The name Omar is of Arabic and Hebrew origin. The meaning of Omar is "speaker, long-lived". The name is a variation of Umar, or from Hebrew meaning 'eloquent'. A Biblical name: the son of Esau, a sheik of Edom. Omar Khayyam (12th century) was an astronomer, a mathematician and also a poet.

Orlando

Pronunciation: or-LAHN-doh

Orlando is of Spanish origin. The name is an Italian form of Roland (Old German). The name means "renowned land".

Orson

Pronunciation: OR-sun

The name Orson is of Latin origin. The meaning of Orson is "bear". Old French ourson, meaning 'little bear.' In medieval French legend, the name was borne by the twin brother of Valentine. The children were sons of an exiled Byzantine Princess. Orson was carried off by a bear as a baby and reared by bears in the forest. Director and Actor Orson Welles (1915-1985) made the name popular.

Oscar

Pronunciation: OS-ker

Oscar is of Old English origin. The meaning of the name Oscar is "spear of the gods". The name was used by Scottish writer, James Macpherson (1736-17-96) for the son of Ossian in his Ossian poems. Napoleon Bonaparte was a great admirer of Macpherson's work, and later gave the name to his godson. He ascended the throne of Sweden as Oscar I.

Oswald

Pronunciation: OZ-wild

The name Oswald is of Old German origin. The meaning of Oswald is "God's power". From an Old English name, from os, 'god', and weald, 'rule'. The Shropshire town of Oswestry is said to have been named after a 7th-century saint and king of Northumbria borne with the name. The name Oswald was popular during the Middle Ages. Diminutives: Oz, Ozzie, Ozzy.

Otto

Pronunciation: AW-toh

Otto is of Old German origin. The meaning of the name Otto is "wealth". A modification of a common element of Old German names, od, meaning 'prosperity.' Borne by four Holy Roman Emperors. The name became less popular in Britain after the Middle Ages.

Owen

Pronunciation: OH-en

The name Owen is of Scottish and Greek origin. The meaning of Owen is "born of youth". The name is a variant of the Latin name Euenuis. Borne in Welsh legend by several important figures. One being, Owen Glendower (1359-1416). He fought unsuccessfully for Welsh independence from England. The name has huge popularity in Wales.

P

Pablo

Pronunciation: PAB-low
The name Pablo is of Spanish origin. The
meaning of Pablo is "little". The name is a
variant of Paul. Borne by artist Pablo
Picasso (1881-1973).

Pacifico

Pronunciation: PAS-if-i-co
The name Pacifico is of Spanish and Latin
origin. The meaning of Pacifico is "calm,
tranquil".

Palmer

Pronunciation: PAHL-mer
The name Palmer is of Old English origin.
The meaning of Palmer is "Pilgrim".
Originally a surname used to refer to the
palm branch carried by a Christian pilgrim,
while they traveled to a holy shrine.

Paris

Pronunciation: PARE-iss
The name Paris is of Greek origin. In Greek
mythology, Paris was the name of the
young prince of Troy, whose love affair
with Helen caused the Trojan war. Paris is
used as both a boy's name, and as a girl's
name. The name was also an English given
surname for immigrants from the capital of
France.

Parker

Pronunciation: PAR-ker
Parker is of Old English origin. The
meaning of Parker is "park keeper".
Originally an occupational name, that was
used as a surname. Parker became a
popular given name in the 19th century.

Parry

Pronunciation: PAR-ry
The name Parry is of Old Welsh origin. The
meaning of Parry is "son of Harry". The
name is also an English variant of Perry.

Patrick

Pronunciation: PAT-rik
The name Patrick is of Latin origin. The
meaning of Patrick is "patrician". St.
Patrick (c. 389-461) was a Briton and a
Roman citizen who traveled as a missionary
to Ireland. After he arrived in Wicklow in
432, he is credited with converting almost
the entire country to Christianity. St Patrick
is also renowned for ridding Ireland of
snakes and vermin. He is the patron saint of
Ireland; his feast day is 17th March. The
name spread outside of Ireland in the 18th
century.

Paul

Pronunciation: pahl
Paul is of Latin origin. The meaning of the
name Paul is "small". From the Roman
family name Paulus, originally from paulus,
'small'. Borne by Saul of Tarsus (Acts 13:9),
he was a Roman citizen and persecutor of
Christians until his conversion. As St Paul,
he is considered to be the co-founder of the
Christian Church with St Peter.

Perceval

Pronunciation: PER-ce-val
The name Perceval is of Old French origin.
The meaning of Perceval is "pierce the
vale". From Old French perce, 'pierce', and
val, 'valley'. Invented by a medieval poet,

Chretien de Troyes in his 12th-century accounts of Arthurian legend.

Percy

Pronunciation: PER-see

Percy is of Latin origin. The meaning of the name Percy is "to penetrate the hedge". Percy is an adopted aristocratic surname, born by the Duke of Northumberland. Derived from the Old French perce, 'piece', and haie, 'hedge'.

Peter

Pronunciation: PEE-tar

The name Peter is of Greek origin. The meaning of Peter is "rock". A biblical name: borne as one of the twelve apostles. The name was given to his apostle Simon by Jesus. Peter, the fisherman, was impulsive and had a strong faith. "Thou art Peter, and upon this rock I will build my church" (Matthew 16:18). St Peter is considered to be one of the co-founders of the Christian Church with St Paul. In the Catholic tradition the first Bishop of Rome and the first pope. Peter is considered the patron saint of fisherman; his feast day is 29th June. J M Barrie's play Peter Pan (1904) revived the name and made it more popular.

Philip

Pronunciation: FIL-ip

The name Philip is of Greek origin. The meaning of Philip is "horse lover". The Greek name Philipos, which means 'lover of horses.' A biblical name; borne by one of Christ's twelve apostles and several early saints. Philip has been in regular use since the early Christian times. St Philip the Apostle's feast day is 1st May.

Piers

Pronunciation: PEE-ers

The name Piers if of Greek origin. The meaning of Piers is "rock". French medieval vernacular form of the name Peter. The name was introduced to Britain by the Normans in the Middle Ages.

Plantagenet

Pronunciation: P-lanta-genet

Plantagenet is of Old French origin. The meaning of the name Plantagenet is "shoot of broom". The name was commonly given to the English royal line from Henry II to Richard III. Broom is an English flower.

Porter

Pronunciation: PORT-er

The name Porter is of English origin. The meaning of Porter is "gatekeeper". Originally an English occupational name and given surname. Porter is also a French name given to people who made their living carrying loads. The French meaning of Porter is "to carry".

Presley

Pronunciation: PRES-ley

Presley is of Old English origin. The meaning of the name Presley is "priest's meadow". The name has been used since the Middle Ages. Presley is also a place name. The name was made famous by the singer Elvis Presley.

Preston
Pronunciation: PRES-ten
The name Preston is of Old English origin. The meaning of Preston is "priest's settlement". Preston is also a place name.

Price
Pronunciation: PRI-ce
The name Price is of Old French origin. The meaning of Price is "prize".

Purvis
Pronunciation: PUR-vis
The name Purvis if of English and French origin. The meaning of Purvis is "purveyor". Originally a term for someone who provides food and provisions.

Q

Qasim

Pronunciation: KA-sim

The name Qasim is of Arabic origin. The meaning of Qasim is "charitable, generous".

Quade

Pronunciation: kwayde

The name Quade is of Gaelic origin. The meaning of Quade is unknown. The name is derived from a Scottish clan name McQuade.

Quanah

Pronunciation: KWAH-ne

The name Quanah is of Native American Indian origin. The meaning of Quanah is "sweet-smelling". The name was borne by a 19th-century chief of the Comanche.

Quennell

Pronunciation: KWEN-el

The name Quennell is of Old French origin. The meaning of Quennell is "small oak". Originally a place name.

Quentin

Pronunciation: KWEN-tin

The name Quentin is of Latin origin. The meaning of Quentin is "fifth". Old French form of the Latin name Quintius, from quintus, 'fifth'. It was the name of a 3rd-century saint and missionary to Gaul.

Quigley

Pronunciation: KWIG-lee

The name Quigley is of Irish and Gaelic origin. The meaning of Quigley is "one with messy hair".

Quillan

Pronunciation: KWIL-an

The name Quillan is of Irish and Gaelic origin. The meaning of Quillan is "cub".

Quimby

Pronunciation: KWIM-bee

Quimby is of Old Norse origin. The meaning of Quimby is "estate of the woman". Quimby is also a place name.

Quincey

Pronunciation: KWIN-cey

Quincey is of Old French origin. The meaning of the name Quincey is "Estate of the fifth son". Adopted surname, originally a baronial name from Cuinchy in northern France. Quincey can be used as a both a boy's name, and as a girl's name.

Quinn

Pronunciation: KWIN

The name Quinn is of Irish and Gaelic origin. The meaning of Quinn is "counsel". An adopted Irish surname, from the Gaelic name O Cuinn, meaning 'decedent of Conn.' Quinn has been used a given name from very ancient times.

Quintin

Pronunciation: KWIN-tin

Quintin is of Old English origin. The meaning of the name Quintin is "fifth". The name is a variant of Quentin. Quintin is an adopted surname and a place name, from Old English cwen, 'queen' and tun, 'settlement'. Diminutive: Quent, Quint.

Quinton

Pronunciation: KWIN-ton

The name Quinton is of Old English origin. The meaning of Quinton is "Queens settlement". Originally a place name.

Quintus

Pronunciation: KWIN-tus

The name Quintus is of Latin origin. The meaning of Quintus is "fifth". The Roman name was often given to the fifth born son, in the days of large families. Quintus is a variant of Quentin. Diminutive: Quent, Quint.

Quintrell

Pronunciation: kwin-TREL

The name Quintrell is of English origin. The meaning of Quintrell is "dashing, elegant".

R

Ralph

Pronunciation: RAL-f
The name Ralph is of French origin. The meaning of Ralph is "counsel". From the Norman French name Raulf.

Ramsey

Pronunciation: RAM-see
Ramsey is of Old English origin. The meaning of the name Ramsey is "raven island". An adopted Scottish surname, which was originally derived from the Huntingdonshire town of Ramsey. Earl of Huntington brought the name to Scotland in the 12th century.

Ranald

Pronunciation: RAN-ald
The name Ranald is of Scottish origin. The meaning of Ranald is unknown. The name is an anglicised form of Raghnall.

Randall

Pronunciation: RAN-dall
The name Randall is of Old English origin. The meaning of Randall is unknown. The name is a medieval form of Randolf. Diminutives: Ran, Randy.

Randolf

Pronunciation: RAN-dolf
The name Randolf is of Old Norse origin. The meaning of Randolf is "shield, wolf". From the Old Norse name Rannulfr. Diminutives: Ran, Randy.

Raoul

Pronunciation: RA-oul
The name Raoul is of French origin. The meaning of Raoul is "wolf counsel". The name is a French form of Ralph. The name was popular in medieval Britain.

Ravi

Pronunciation: RAV-ee
The name Ravi is of Indian origin. The meaning of Ravi is "sun". Ravi was the name of the sun god.

Raymond

Pronunciation: RAY-mund
The name Raymond is of Old German origin. The meaning of Raymond is "protecting hand". From the Old French name Raimund. The name was borne by an 11th-century Count who was a Crusader leader of the First Crusade. The name was introduced to Britain by the Normans. Diminutive: Ray.

Rayner

Pronunciation: RAY-ner
The name Rayner is of Old German origin. The meaning of Rayner is "judgment warrior". The name was introduced to Britain by the Normans.

Reuben

Pronunciation: ROO-ben
The name Reuben is of Hebrew origin. The meaning of Reuben is "Behold, a son". A biblical name: borne by the firstborn of Jacob's twelve sons.

Rex

Pronunciation: reks
The name Res is of Latin origin. The meaning of Rex is "king". The name is also

considered a diminutive of Reginald.

Rhys

Pronunciation: rees

Rhys is of Welsh origin. The meaning of the name Rhys is "passion, enthusiasm". Rhys is a native Welsh form of Reece. The name was borne by two medieval Welsh lords.

Richard

Pronunciation: RICH-erd

The name Richard is of Old German origin. The meaning of Richard is "powerful leader". From an Old German name Ricohard. Diminutives: Rick, Dickie, Dickon, Dicky, Rich, Richie, Rick, Ricky.

Ridley

Pronunciation: RID-lee

The name Ridley is of Old English origin. The meaning of Ridley is "reed meadow". Originally an adopted surname and place name, from Old English elements hreod.

River

Pronunciation: RIV-er

The name River is of English origin. The name was popular during the 1960's when people took names from nature. Hollywood actor, River Phoenix (1970-1993) popularised name.

Roald

Pronunciation: ROH-al

The name Roald is of Old Norse origin. The meaning of Roald is "famous ruler, famed power". The name was made famous by the writer Roald Dahl.

Robert

Pronunciation: RAH-bert

Robert is of Old German origin. The meaning of the name Robert is "bright fame". From the Old German name Hrodebert. The name was introduced to Britain by the Normans. Robert has been a popular boys name since the Middle Ages. King Robert the Bruce (1274-1329) popularised the name in Scotland. Diminutives: Bob, Bobbie, Bobby, Hob, Rab, Rabbie, Rob, Robbie, Robby.

Robin

Pronunciation: RAH-bin

The name Robin is of English origin. The meaning of Robin is unknown. Robyn is originally a diminutive of Robert. The name has been popular since the medieval days of Robin Hood.

Roderick

Pronunciation: RAH-der-ik

The name Roderick is of Old German origin. The meaning of Roderick is "famous power". The name was first introduced to Britain by the Norman invaders. The name was revived by Sir Walter Scott in his poem The Vision of Don Roderigo (1811). Diminutives: Rod, Rody.

Rodney

Pronunciation: RAHD-nee

Rodney is of Old English and Old German origin. The meaning of the name Rodney is "Roda's island". An adopted surname and place name. It was originally adopted in honour of Admiral Lord Rodney (1719-1792), who led the French Navy to defeat in 1759. Diminutives: Rod, Roddy.

Roger

Pronunciation: ROH-jer

The name Roger is of Old German origin. The meaning of Roger is "famous spearman". From the Old French name Rogier, which is derived from Old German hrod. The name was introduced to Britain by the Normans. Roger was a popular name throughout the Middle Ages and in the 19th and 20th centuries.

Roland

Pronunciation: ROH-land

The name Roland is of Old German origin. The meaning of Roland is "renowned land". Roland is rejoiced in the 12th-century French poetic sagas, Chanson de Roland, as a hero in the service of Charlemagne. He was the most famous of Charlemagne's soldiers, who died c. 778. Roland is also known as the Christian Theseus and the Achilles of the West. Roland is an anglicised form of the name Rowland. The name was introduced to Britain by the Normans. Diminutive: Roly.

Rollo

Pronunciation: ROH-llo

The name Rollo is of Latin origin. The meaning of Rollo is unknown. Rollo is a Latin form of the name Roul. The name was borne by an ancestor of William the Conqueror and a Norman pirate (c. 860-932).

Roman

Pronunciation: roh-MAHN

The name Roman is of Latin origin. The meaning of Roman is "citizen of Rome". Roman is an anglicised form of the name Romeo. The name is also a variant of Romanus, the name of several saints and a pope.

Romeo

Pronunciation: ROAM-ee-ohh

Romeo is of Latin origin. The meaning of the name Romeo is "citizen of Rome". The name was made famous by Shakespeare's Romeo and Juliet (1595).

Ronald

Pronunciation: RAH-nald

The name Ronald is of Old Norse origin. The meaning of Ronald is "ruler's counselor". The name was revived in the 19th century. Diminutives: Ron, Ronnie.

Rory

Pronunciation: ROR-ee

The name Rory is of Irish and Gaelic origin. The meaning of Rory is "red king". The name is an anglicised form of the Irish Gaelic names Ruaidhrí, Ruarí, and Scottish Gaelic names, Ruairidh, Ruaraidh.

Ross

Pronunciation: ros

Ross is of Scottish and Gaelic origin. The meaning of the name Ross is "headland, cape". Derived from Scottish Gaelic ros, meaning 'headland.' Ross is an adopted surname and place name.

Rowan
Pronunciation: RO-wan
The name Rowan is of Gaelic origin. The meaning of Rowan is "little red-haired one". An adopted Irish surname. Borne by a 6th-century saint who founded the monastery of Lothar.

Roy
Pronunciation: roy
The name Roy is of Irish and Gaelic origin. The meaning of Roy is "red". From Scottish Gaelic, ruadh. The name was also influenced by the Old French term roi, which means 'king.'

Rudolf
Pronunciation: ROO-dol-f
The name Rudolf is of Latin origin. The meaning of Rudolf is "famous wolf". From Rudolphus, the Latinate form of Hrodwulf. Diminutives: Rudi, Rudy.

Rufus
Pronunciation: ROO-fuss
The name Rufus is of Latin origin. The meaning of Rufus is "red-haired". Rufus was first used as a first name during the 19th century. A biblical name; borne by the name of two 1st century Christians.

Rupert
Pronunciation: ROO-pert
The name Rupert is of Old German origin. The meaning of Rupert is unknown. From Rupprecht, a German form of Robert. The name was popularised throughout Britain by Prince Rupert of the Rhine (1618-1692). He was the nephew of Charles I. St Rupert of Salzburg of the 8th century was involved in the founding of Salzburg.

Russell
Pronunciation: RUSS-el
Russell is of Old French origin. The meaning of the name Russell is "little red". Russell is an adopted surname from Old French roux. The name was first used as a first name in the 19th century. Diminutives: Russ.

Ryan
Pronunciation: RYE-an
The name Ryan is of Gaelic origin. The meaning of Ryan is "king". From the Irish Gaelic surname O'Riain, which means 'a descendant of Rian.'

S

Saahdia

Pronunciation: sa(ah)-dia

The name Saahdia is of Aramaic origin. The meaning of Saahdia is "the Lord's help".

Saarik

Pronunciation: sa(a)-rik

The name Saarik is of Hindi origin. The meaning of Saarik is unknown. Saarik is also the name of a small songbird.

Saber

Pronunciation: S-(a)-ber

The name Saber is of French origin. The meaning of Saber is "sword". Saber is the name of a curved sword.

Sabino

Pronunciation: sa-BEE-noh

Sabino is of Latin origin. The meaning of the name Sabino is "Sabine". The Sabines were a tribe from Italy. Romulus arranged for the Sabine women to be kidnapped, and provided as wives for the citizens of Rome. Sabino is also a saint's name.

Sacha

Pronunciation: S(a)-cha

The name Sacha is of Greek and Russian origin. The meaning of Sacha is "man's defender". The name is used as both a boy's name, and as a girl's name. Sacha is a diminutive of Alexander.

Sadiki

Pronunciation: S(a)-dee-kee

The name Sadiki is of Swahili origin. The meaning of Sadiki is "faithful, loyal".

Sadler

Pronunciation: SAD-ler

Sadler is of Old English origin. The meaning of the name Sadler is "harness maker". Originally a surname and occupational name. The name was first used as a first name in the 19th century.

Safford

Pronunciation: SAFF-ord

Safford is of Old English origin. The meaning of the name Safford is "willow river crossing". Originally a place name.

Saffron

Pronunciation: SAFF-ron

Saffron is the name of a plant. Saffron is used as a bright orange/yellow spice. Saffron is the most expensIve of all spices. Derived from Arabic, zafaran. The name is used as both a boy's name, and as a girl's name.

Sage

Pronunciation: sage

The name Sage is of Latin origin. The meaning of Sage is "healing herb". Sage is also the name of a plant. The name is used as both a boy's name. and as a girl's name.

Sahil

Pronunciation: SA-hill

The name Sahil is of Hindi origin. The meaning of Sahil is "leader".

Salvador

Pronunciation: SAL-va-dor

The name Salvador is of Latin origin. The meaning of Salvador is "savior".

The name is a Spanish form of Salvator. Salvador is a place name in Latin America.

Samuel

Pronunciation: SAM-yoo-el

The name Samuel is of Hebrew origin. The meaning of Samuel is "God has heard". A biblical name; borne in the Old Testament as the prophet and judge who anointed Saul and David as kings of Israel (1 and 2 Samuel). The name was used by the Puritans. Samuel was a popular name throughout the 17th, 18th, and 19th centuries. The diminutive, Sam is one of the most popular boy's names in the English-speaking world. Diminutives: Sam, Sammie, Sammy.

Scott

Pronunciation: skaht

Scott is of Old English origin. The meaning of the name Scott is "from Scotland, a Scotsman". An adopted Scottish surname, the name has been in regular use since the early 20th century. American writer, F Scott Fitzgerald (1896-1940) popularised the name.

Sean

Pronunciation: shon

The name Sean is of Irish and Hebrew origin. The meaning of Sean is "God is gracious". The name is an Irish form of John, derived from the French form Jean. The name spread outside of Ireland in the 20th century.

Sebastian

Pronunciation: se-BASS-tian

Sebastian is of Greek origin. The meaning of the name Sebastian is "man of Sebastia". From the Latin name Sebastianus. The original form of the name referred to those from a particular city or region of Asia Minor. Borne by an early Roman soldier who converted to Christianity, his fellow officers tried to kill him with arrows. St Sebastian was a 3rd century martyred centurion who became the patron saint of soldiers. Shakespeare used the name for the twin brother of Viola in Twelfth Night (1601). Diminutives: Bastian, Bastien, Seb.

Seth

Pronunciation: seth

The name Seth is of Hebrew origin. The meaning of Seth is "set, appointed". A biblical name: borne in the Old Testament by the third son of Adam and Eve as a replacement for their dead son. Eve said Seth had been appointed to take the place of Abel, who had been killed by Cain. The name was popular with the Puritans of the 17th century.

Seymour

Pronunciation: SEE-mor

The name Seymour is of English origin. The meaning of Seymour is "Saint Maur". An adopted aristocratic surname and French place name from St Maur in France. The Norman French name Maur is derived from the Latin name Mauricius. The name has been in use as a first name since the 19th century.

Shane

Pronunciation: shayn

The name Shane is of Irish and Hebrew origin. The meaning of Shane is "God is gracious". The name is a variation of Sean. The name became more popular during the 1950's and 1960's due to the classic western film Shane (1953).

Sheldon

Pronunciation: SHEL-den

The name Sheldon is of Old English origin. The meaning of Sheldon is "steep valley". The adopted surname is derived from various English place names, including 'flat-topped hill'.

Sheridan

Pronunciation: SHARE-a-den

The name Sheridan is of Irish and Gaelic origin. The meaning of Sheridan is "seeker". An adopted Irish surname, from O Sirideain. The name was popularised by Irish playwright Richard Brinsley Sheridan (1751-1861). The name is used as both a boy's name and as a girl's name.

Sidney, Sydney

Pronunciation: SID-nee

Sidney is of Old English origin. The meaning of the name Sidney is "wide meadow". Sidney is an adopted surname and place name. The name has been used as a first name since the 17th century. Charles

Dickens boosted the popularity of the name when he used it for his hero in A Tale Of Two Cities (1859). The Australian city of Sydney was named in honour of Thomas Townshend. The name is used as both a boy's name, and as a girl's name.

Silvester

Pronunciation: SIL-vest-er

The name Silvester is of Latin origin. The meaning of Silvester is "of the woods". The name was borne by an early Christian martyr and three popes.

Simon

Pronunciation: SYE-mun

The name Simon is of Hebrew origin. The meaning of Simon is "to hear, to be heard". The name is a variation of Simeon. A biblical name; borne in the New Testament by several characters. Simon was the name of two of the apostles, Simon Peter and Simon the Zealot. The name was popular from the Middle Ages through to the 18th century.

Sinclair

Pronunciation: sin-KLARE

Sinclair is of English origin. The meaning of the name Sinclair is "from Saint Clair". The name is an adopted Scottish surname, derived from a French baronial name and place name.

Sky

Pronunciation: SKY

The name Sky is of English origin. The meaning of Sky is unknown. The name is a variant of Skye. Sky is also used as a nickname for the Skyler variant. The name was popular during the 1960's when people took names from nature.

Solomon

Pronunciation: SAH-lah-mun

Solomon is of Hebrew origin. The meaning of the name Solomon is "peace". A biblical name; borne in the Old Testament by a king of Israel, the son of David and Bathsheba. He was known for his wisdom and justice and wrote the Book of Proverbs. Solomon was a popular name during the Middle Ages; the name was revived in the 17th century.

Spencer

Pronunciation: SPEN-ser

The name Spencer is of Middle English origin. The meaning of Spencer is "dispenser of provisions". The adopted aristocratic surname was originally an occupational name for a steward or butler. The name has been associated with the Churchill family, Dukes of Marlborough since the 18th century.

Stafford

Pronunciation: STAFF-ord

The name Stafford is of Old English origin. The meaning of Stafford is "Ford by a landing place". An adopted aristocratic surname and English place name. Stafford has been in occasional use as a first name since the mid-19th century.

Stanford

Pronunciation: STAN-ford

Stanford is of Old English origin. The meaning of the name Stanford is "stoney ford". Stanford is also a place name.

Stanley

Pronunciation: STAN-lee

The name Stanley is of Old English origin. The meaning of Stanley is "stony meadow". Stanley is an adopted surname and place name. The name was first used as a first name in the 19th century. Diminutive: Stan.

Stephen

Pronunciation: STEE-ven

The name Stephen is of Greek origin. The meaning of Stephen is "garland, crown". From Greek stephanos, which means 'crown.' St Stephen was the first person to be martyred for his Christian faith. Accused of blasphemy, he was stoned to death by the Jews (Acts 6-8). The name was borne by several saints and ten popes. The name was introduced to Britain by the Normans. Diminutives: Steve, Stevie.

Stewart

Pronunciation: STOO-ert

The name Stewart is of Old English origin. The meaning of Stewart is "steward". The name is an early variant of Stuart. Stewart was the family name of the royal house of Scotland from 1371 to 1714, and of England from 1603. Originally an occupational name, a medieval steward was charged with the care of the castle and estate affairs. Diminutives: Stew, Stu.

Stuart

Pronunciation: STU-art

Stuart is of Old English origin. The meaning of the name Stuart is "steward". Originally an occupational name, the steward administers a large feudal household. The name was introduced by Mary Queen of Scots. Stuart and Steward are clan names of the royal house of Scotland. Diminutives: Stew, Stu.

Sullivan

Pronunciation: SIL-IH-VUN

The name Sullivan is of Gaelic origin. The meaning of Sullivan is "dark eyes".

T

Tabor

Pronunciation: TAY-bor

The name Tabor is of Hebrew and Hungarian origin. The meaning of Tabor is "misfortune, bad luck". A biblical name; Mount Tabor a landmark mountain near Nazareth.

Tad

Pronunciation: tad

The name Tad is of English origin. The meaning of Tad is "heart". The name is a diminutive of Tadhg or Thaddeus. Tad is also used in American slang meaning, 'small'.

Tadhg

Pronunciation: teig

The name Tadhg is of Irish, Gaelic, and Scottish origin. The meaning of Tadhg is "poet, philosopher".

Talfryn

Pronunciation: tal-(f)-ryn

The name Talfryn is of Welsh origin. The meaning of Talfryn is "high hill".

Taliesin

Pronunciation: TAL-ie-sin

The name Taliesin is of Welsh origin. The meaning of Taliesin is "shining forehead". Borne by a 6th century Welsh poet.

Tam

Pronunciation: TAM

Tam is of Aramaic origin. The meaning of the name Tam is "twin". The name is a variant of Thomas. A biblical name: borne by one of the twelve apostles, he is also known as 'doubting Thomas.'

Tancred

Pronunciation: TAN-cred

The name Tancred is of Old German origin. The meaning of Tancred is "counsel, advice". Tancred was an 11th century Norman Knight and Crusader; he was the son of Otho the Good and Emma Guiscard. He appears as one of the leading characters in the Italian Torquato Tasso's poem, Jerusalem Delivered (1581). He also inspired Rossini's opera Tancredi (1813) and Disraeli's novel Tancred (1847). The name was introduced to Britain by the Normans.

Terence

Pronunciation: TARE-ence

The name Terence is of Latin origin. The meaning of Terence is "one who initiates an idea". Latin from the Roman family name, Terentius. Diminutives: Tel, Terry.

Theobald

Pronunciation: THEE-o-bald

The name Theobald is of Old German origin. The meaning of Theobald is "brave people". Diminutive: Theo.

Theodore

Pronunciation: THEE-a-dor

Theodore is of Greek origin. The meaning of name Theodore is "God's gift". Theodore is an early Christian name and a saint's name. The name became popular after a stuffed toy bear was named Teddy in honour of the US president, Theodore Roosevelt (1858-1919). Diminutives: Ted,

Teddie, Teddy, Theo.

Theodoric

Pronunciation: THEE-o-dor-ic

The name Theodoric is of Old German origin. The meaning of Theodoric is "people's ruler, leader of the people". The name was borne by a king of the Ostrogoths (c. 454-526) who invaded Italy.
Diminutives: Derek, Derrick, Theo.

Thomas

Pronunciation: TAH-mas

Thomas is of Aramaic origin. The meaning of Thomas is "twin". A biblical name; borne by one of the twelve apostles also known as 'doubting Thomas.' The Apocrypha's Acts of Thomas tells of the apostle's missionary work in India. His feast day is 3rd July. Diminutives: Tom, Tommie, Tommy, Tam.

Thorley

Pronunciation: THOR-lee

The name Thorley is of Old English origin. The meaning of Thorley is "Thor's meadow, Thor's wood". Thorley is also a place name.

Thurston

Pronunciation: THER-sten

The name Thurston is of Old English origin. The meaning of Thurston is "Thor's stone".

Tierney

Pronunciation: TIE-r-ney

The name Tierney is of Irish and Gaelic origin. The meaning of Tierney is "Lord". An adopted surname from the Irish Galic name Ó Tighearnaigh.

Timothy

Pronunciation: TIM-oh-thee

Timothy is of Greek origin. The meaning of the name Timothy is "God's honor". A biblical name; born by a young Christian who was a companion of St Paul. Timothy is derived from the Greek name Timotheos. Charles Dickens popularised the name in the 19th century with his novel, A Christmas Carol (1843). Diminutives: Tim, Timmie, Timmy.

Tobias

Pronunciation: TOB-ias

The name Tobias is of Hebrew origin. The meaning of Tobias is "God is good". A biblical name; borne in the Old Testament Apocrypha's Book of Tobit, Tibias, was accompanied on a journey to Ecbatana by the Archangel Raphael. The name was used by the Puritans and later revived in the 19th century.

Todd

Pronunciation: tahd

The name Todd is of Middle English origin. The meaning of Todd is "Fox". The name was possibly used to refer to a fox hunter, or to indicate colouring, or cunning. Todd is an adopted surname.

Torquil
Pronunciation: TOR-quil
The name Torquil is of Gaelic and Scottish origin. The meaning of Torquil is "Thor's helmet". Scottish Gaelic, from porketil, por being a contraction of Thor (the Norse god of thunder). Ketil meaning, 'cauldron'. Thor's cauldron was an instrument used for sacrifices. The name was introduced to Britain by the Vikings.

Traherne
Pronunciation: TRA-herne
The name Traherne is of Welsh origin. The meaning of Traherne is "strength of iron, greatly akin to iron". The name is a variant form of Welsh Trahaearn.

Travers
Pronunciation: TRAV-ers
The name Travers is of Old French origin. The meaning of Travers is "to cross over". An adopted surname from Old French travers, meaning 'crossing.' Originally an occupational surname which was given to gatekeepers and others who collected tolls at bridges.

Travis
Pronunciation: TRAV-iss.
Travis is of Old French origin. The meaning of the name Travis is "to cross over". An adopted surname from Old French travers, meaning 'crossing.' Travis was an occupational surname given to gatekeepers and others who collected tolls

at bridges.

Tremaine
Pronunciation: TRE-maine
Tremaine is of English origin. The meaning of Tremaine is "town built with stone". The name is a variant of Tremain. Tremaine is an adopted Cornish surname.

Trevor
Pronunciation: TREV-or
The name Trevor is of Welsh origin. The meaning of Trevor is "great settlement". Trevor is an adopted Welsh surname.

Tristan
Pronunciation: TRISS-tan
The name Tristan is of Celtic origin. The name is influenced by Old French triste, from Latin tristis, meaning 'sad.' Borne in Arthurian legend as a Knight of the Round Table and the tragic hero of the medieval tale, Tristan, and Isolde. Tristan was a hero of Celtic legend and medieval romance.

Troy
Pronunciation: TR-oy
The name Troy is of Irish and Gaelic origin. The meaning of Troy is "descendant of the footsoldier". An adopted surname which was given to those who migrated to England from Troyes in France, after the Norman conquest of 1066. Troy is also associated with the ancient city in Asia Minor where the Trojan wars were fought. The name is used as both a boy's name, and as a girl's name.

Tyrone

Pronunciation: TY-rohn

The name Tyrone is of Gaelic origin. The meaning of Tyrone is "land of Eoghan". An adopted surname derived from the Northern Ireland county of Tyrone.

Diminutive: Ty.

U

Ulises

Pronunciation: u-li-ses

Ulises is a variant of the Latin name
Ulysses, a variant of the Greek name
Odysseus, which means "wrathful."

Ulick

Pronunciation: u-li-ck

The name Ulick is of Irish and Gaelic
origin. The meaning of the name Ulick is
"little William".

Ulysses

Pronunciation: you-LISS-ees

Ulysses is of Latin origin, a variant of the
Greek name Odysseus, which means
"wrathful." Ulysses was an intelligent and
resourceful hero of Homer's epic Odyssey.

Umar

Pronunciation: u-mar

The name Umar is of Arabic origin. The
meaning of the name is "flourishing".
Borne by a lifelong companion of the
Prophet Muhammad.

Umberto

Pronunciation: um-ber-to

Umberto is of Italian origin. The name is a
variant of the Old German name, Humbert
which means "renowned hun." Umberto is
a royal name in Italy.

Upton

Pronunciation: Up-ton

Upton is an adopted surname and a place
name. The name is of Old English origin,
from up, "higher" and tun, "settlement".

The meaning of the name Upton is "upper
settlement".

Urban

Pronunciation: ur-ban

Urban is of Latin origin, from urbanus
which means, "citizen." The meaning of
Urban is "from the city". A biblical name;
borne by a character in the New Testament.
Urban is also the name of eight popes.

Uriah

Pronunciation: yer-RY-ah

The name Uriah is of Hebrew origin. The
meaning of the name Uriah is "my light is
Jehovah". A biblical name; borne in the Old
Testament one of King David's warriors.
He was the husband of Bathsheba, who was
sent to certain death in battle by David.

Uriel

Pronunciation: OOR-ee-el

Uriel is of Hebrew origin. The meaning of
the name is "angel of light", "flame of
God". In the Apocrypha, Uriel is one of the
seven archangels.

Urijah

Pronunciation: u-ri-jah

Urijah is a variant of the Hebrew name
Uriah. The meaning of the name Urijah is
"my light is Jehovah". A biblical name;
borne of one of King David's warriors, and
the husband of Bathsheba.

Uziel

Pronunciation: u-ziel

The name Uziel is of Hebrew origin. The
meaning of the name is "strength",
"power".

V

Vachel

Pronunciation: VAY-chel

The name Vachel is of Old French origin. The meaning of Vachel is "small cow".

Vail

Pronunciation: VAY-el

The name Vail is of Old English origin. The meaning of Vail is "Valley". Originally a place name.

Valen

Pronunciation: VA-len

Valen is a variant of the Latin name Valentine. The meaning of the name Valen is "strong", "healthy". Valen is used as a both a boy's name, and as a girl's name.

Valentine

Pronunciation: VAL-en-tyne

Valentine is of Latin origin. The meaning of Valentine is "strong", "healthy". Valentine is also a variant of Valentinus, which was the name of more than 50 saints and three Roman emperors.

Van

Pronunciation: van

The name Van is of Danish origin. The name is a diminutive of Ewan and Ivan. It is also a nickname for Evan. The adopted surname was introduced as a given name by early immigrants in America.

Vance

Pronunciation: vance

The name Vance is of Old English origin. The meaning of the name Vance is "marshland".

Varun

Pronunciation: va-run

The name Varun is of Hindi origin. The meaning of Varun is "water god".

Vaughn

Pronunciation: von

The name Vaughn is of Welsh origin. The adopted surname was first used as a given first name in the early 20th century. The meaning of the name Vaughn is "little" taken from fychan, meaning "small."

Vere

Pronunciation: v (e)-re

Vere is of French origin. Vere is an adopted surname and French Baronial name. It is also an upper-class surname in England. Derived from Old French vern which means, "alder."

Vernon

Pronunciation: VER-non

Vernon is of Old French origin. Derived from Old French vern which means, "alder." The meaning of the name is "alder grove". The aristocratic surname was brought to England by the Norman conquest. Richard de Vernon arrived in Britain with William the Conqueror in 1066. Vernon is also a place name.

Vicente

Pronunciation: VICE-nte

Vicente is a variant of the Latin name Vincent. The meaning of the name Vicente is "prevailing".

Victor

Pronunciation: VIK-tor

The name Victor is of Latin origin. The meaning of the name Victor is "Champion". Victor is a very popular saint's name, common in Christian Rome.

Vincent

Pronunciation: VIN-sent

Vincent is of Latin origin. The meaning of Vincent is "prevailing". Derived from Latin vincens, meaning "conquering." Borne by several early saints and steadily used since the early Christian days. Saint Vincent of Saragossa was a 4th-century Spanish martyr. Saint Vincent de Paul, a 17th-century priest. The name was popular during the Middle Ages and was revived during the 19th century.

Virgil

Pronunciation: VER-jil

Virgil is of Latin origin from vergilius. Anglicized form of the name of the Roman poet and philosopher, Publius Vergilius Maro. Regarded as one of the greatest poets of ancient Rome, he was considered to have had magical powers and many medieval romances the poems tell of his exploits. His work has been used to study Roman history and the Latin language for the past two-thousand years.

Vitus

Pronunciation: VI-tus

Vitus is a variant of the Latin name Vito.

The meaning of the name is "life-giving".

Vivian

Pronunciation: VIV-ian

The name Vivian is of Latin origin. Old French form of the Latin name Vivianus, from vivus which means "alive," "lively." The meaning of the name Vivian is "full of life" Vivian is used as both a boy's name and as a girl's name.

W

Wade

Pronunciation: wayde

Wade is of Old English and Scandinavian origin. The meaning of the name Wade is "river ford". Wade is also a medieval given name taken from Scandinavian mythology.

Wadham

Pronunciation: WAD-ham

The name Wadham is of Old English origin. The meaning of Wadham is "Ford village". Wadham is also a place name.

Wadley

Pronunciation: WAD-lee

The name Wadley is of Old English origin. The meaning of Wadley is "Ford meadow". Wadley is also a place name.

Wadsworth

Pronunciation: WADS-wor-th

The name Wadsworth is of Old English origin. The meaning of Wadsworth is "village near the ford". Wadsworth is also a place name.

Wagner

Pronunciation: WAG-ner

The name Wagner is of German origin. The meaning of Wagner is "wagon builder". Originally an occupational name.

Wahib

Pronunciation: WA-hib

The name Wahib is of Arabic origin. The meaning of Wahib is "donor". The name is one of Allah's 99 attributes.

Wainwright

Pronunciation: WAYN-ri-ght

The name Wainwright is of Old English origin. The meaning of Wainwright is "wagon builder".

Waite

Pronunciation: WAY-te

The name Waite is of Middle English origin. The meaning of Waite is "guard, watchman". Originally an occupational name. Christmas carolers were known as 'waits.'

Wakeley

Pronunciation: VIV-ian

Wakeley is of Old English origin. The meaning of the name Wakeley is "damp meadow". Wakeley is also a place name.

Walcott

Pronunciation: WALL-cot

The name Walcott is of Old English origin. The meaning of Walcott is "cottage by the wall".

Waldemar

Pronunciation: WALD-e-mar

Waldemar is of Old German origin. The meaning of the name Waldemar is "renowned ruler".

Walden

Pronunciation: WALD-en

The name Walden is of Old English origin. The meaning of Walden is "wooden valley". Walden is also a place name.

Waldo

Pronunciation: WAL-DOH

The name Waldo is of Old German origin. The meaning of the name Waldo is "rule". Derived from a Latinized form of the Old German wald, which means "to rule." Waldo is a short form and diminutive of several Old German names such as Oswald.

Walker

Pronunciation: WAHL-ker

The name Walker is Old English origin. The meaning of the name is "cloth washer", "walker". Walker is an occupational name from the medieval era, were workers trod on fabric to cleanse of any impurities.

Wallace

Pronunciation: WAL-iss

The name Wallace is of Old French origin. The meaning of the name is "Welshman". Wallace is originally a Scottish surname which refers to foreigners. Use as a first name probably began in honour of a 13th-century Scottish hero, William Wallace. He was a Scottish patriot who struggled against King Edward 1.

Walter

Pronunciation: WAL-ter

Walter is of Old German origin. The meaning of the name Walter is "commander of the army". From the Old German wald, which means "power." It was introduced to Britain by the Normans.

Warren

Pronunciation: war-ren

The name Warren is of Old English origin. The meaning of Warren is "watchman". The name is also possibly from the Norman French warrene, which means "stockyard."

Wayne

Pronunciation: wayne

Wayne is an adopted surname of Old English origin. The name was originally given to cart makers or drivers. The meaning of the name Wayne is "wagon builder", "driver". The name was made famous by actor John Wayne (1907-1979).

Wentworth

Pronunciation: WEN-two-rth

The name Wentworth is an adopted surname that is of Old English origin. Wentworth is also a place name from Old English winter, "Winter" and the word, "enclosure". Used as a reference to settlements that was used only during the cold winter months. The meaning of the name is "pale man's settlement".

Wes

Pronunciation: wes

The name Wes is a variant of the Old English name Wesley. It is also a variant of the English surname Westley. The meaning of the name Wes is "western meadow".

Wesley

Pronunciation: WES-lee

Wesley is of Old English origin. The meaning of Wesley is "western meadow".

Wesley is also a place name and a variant of the English surname Westley. The adopted surname was used in honour of 18th-century brothers John and Charles Wesley, founders of the Methodist Church.

West
Pronunciation: we-ST
The name West is a variant of the Old English place name, Westbrook. The place name refers to the location of a person's dwelling. The meaning of the name West is "western stream".

Wilbur
Pronunciation: wil-BUR
Wilbur is an adopted surname from Old English will, meaning "desire" and burh, "fortress."

Wilder
Pronunciation: WILD-er
The name Wilder is of German origin. Originally an occupational name for someone who captures and kills wild animals. The meaning of the name is "Hunter".

Wiley
Pronunciation: WYE-lee
The name Wiley is of Old English origin. The meaning of the name Wiley is "crafty". The name is also possibly a place name of a village and a river in England, "water meadow".

Willard
Pronunciation: WIL-erd
Willard is of Old English origin. The meaning of the name is "strong desire" It is an adopted surname from will, "deserve", and heard, "brave."

William
Pronunciation: WIL-yum
The name William is of Old German origin. From will meaning "desire" and helm, "helmet." The meaning of the name William is "desiring of protection", "determined protector". The name was brought to Britain by the Norman invader William the Conqueror. Three out of four English boys were given some form of the conqueror's name, William. It was probably the first name to enjoy popularity on a mass scale. William became the most popular name in Britain within a century of the Norman Conquest. The name was also borne by four kings of England and has remained a royal name in Britain for nearly one thousand years.

Willie
Pronunciation: WIL-ee
The name Willie is of English origin. Willie is used as both a boy's name, and also as a girl's name.

Wilmer
Pronunciation: WIL-mer
Wilmer is of Old German origin. The meaning of the name Wilmer is "strong

desire".

Windsor

Pronunciation: WIND-sor

Windsor is an adopted surname of Old English origin. The meaning of the name is "riverbank with a winch". From the Old English name Windels-ora, meaning "landing place with a winch." Windsor is also a place name of a town and castle in England. Windsor is the surname of the British royal family.

Winston

Pronunciation: WIN-stun

The name Winston is of Old English origin. The meaning of the name Winston is "joyful stone". Winston is an adopted surname and English place name. From the Old English name Wynn, and tun, "settlement", which means "Wynn's place." Former British prime minister, Sir Winston Churchill was given the name from his family's connections to the region.

Wolfgang

Pronunciation: WOLF-gang

Wolfgang is of Old German origin. The meaning of the name is "traveling wolf". Famous composer, Wolfgang Amadeus Mozart made the name famous in the English-speaking world.

Wyatt

Pronunciation: WY-ut

The name Wyatt is of Old English origin. The meaning of Wyatt is "war strength". Wyatt is an adopted surname from Old English wig meaning, "war" and heard, "hardy."

Wynne

Pronunciation: WYN-ne

The name Wynne comes from the Welsh word, Gwen, which means "fair, holy, blessed, white." The meaning of the name Wynne is "friend". Wynne is also a variant of the name Wynn. Wynne is used as both a boy's name, and as a girl's name.

Wyndham

Pronunciation: WYND-ham

Wyndham is of Old English origin. The meaning of the name is "Wyman's hamlet", "Hamlet near the winding way". Wyndham is an adopted surname and also a place name, it is a contracted form of the Norfolk town Wymondham.

X

Xavi

Pronunciation: X-avi

Xavi is a variant of the name Xavier. The meaning of the name is "new house".

Xander

Pronunciation: ZAN-der

The name Xander is of Greek origin. The meaning of the name Xander is "man's defender". The name is also a short form of Alexander.

Xavier

Pronunciation: ecks-ZAY-vee-er

Xavier is of Basque origin. The meaning of the name is "new house". Saint Francis Xavier (1506-52) was a Jesuit missionary, who took Christianity to Japan and the East Indies. The name is especially popular in Roman Catholic families.

Xenophon

Pronunciation: X-(e)-no-phon

The name Xenophon is of Greek origin. The meaning of Xenophon is "foreign voice". The name was borne by a 4th-century Greek historian.

Xenos

Pronunciation: X-(e)-nos

The name Xenos is of Greek origin. The meaning of Xenos is "hospitality".

Xerxes

Pronunciation: ZURK-seez, Z-uh-rk-sihs

The name Xerxes is of Persian origin. The meaning of the name is "King", "monarch". Several Persian rulers bore the name Xerxes. One of the rulers from the fifth century BC started a war with the Greeks.

Xidorn

Pronunciation: X-(i)-do-rn

The name Xenophon is of American origin. The meaning of Xidorn is "truth seeker".

Xiomar

Pronunciation: zhoh-MAR

Xiomar is of Spanish origin. The meaning of the name Xiomar is "famous in battle". The name is a variant of Geomar.

Y

Yael

Pronunciation: yael

The name Yael is variant of the Hebrew name Jael. The meaning of the name Yael is "mountain goat", "fertile moor". The name is also a variant of the Old English name Yale.

Yannick

Pronunciation: ya-nni-CK

Yannick is a variant of Yann (French, Hebrew). The meaning of the name Yannick is "God is gracious". Yannick is used as both a boy's name, and as a girl's name.

Yasser

Pronunciation: YAS-ser

Yasser is of Arabic origin. The name is a variant of the Arabic name Yasir. The meaning of the name Yasser is "wealthy", "well to do".

Yehudi

Pronunciation: yehu-di, ye-hudi

Yehudi is of Hebrew origin. The meaning of the name is "Judah", "praise".

Yoel

Pronunciation: yoel

Yoel is a variant of the Hebrew name Joel. The meaning of the name Yoel is "Jehovah is the Lord". A biblical name; borne as a prophet and writer of the Book of Joel.

Yorick

Pronunciation: yo-ri-ck

The name Yorick is a variation of Jorck, a Danish form of George. Yorick is of Old English origin, and the meaning of the name is "farmer". Shakespeare used the name for the court jester in Hamlet (1601).

Yosef

Pronunciation: YO-sef

Yosef is a variant of the name Yusuf. The meaning of the name Yosef is "the Lord increases".

Yousef

Pronunciation: you-sef

Yousef is a variant of the Hebrew name Joseph. A biblical name; borne of the son of Jacob, he was sold by his brothers into slavery, and become a supreme power in Egypt. The meaning of the name Yousef is "Jehovah increases".

Yusuf

Pronunciation: yu-suf

Yusuf is variant of the Hebrew name Joseph. The meaning of the name is "the Lord increases".

Yves

Pronunciation: eve

The name Eve is of French origin. The meaning of the name is "yew". The name is a French variation of Ivo, which is drawn from Old German, Ivo. Saint-Yves (14th century) was a French lawyer and a priest. The name is also possibly an occupational name.

Z

Zachariah

Pronunciation: zak-a-RYE-ah

Zachariah is of Hebrew origin. The meaning of Zachariah is "the Lord recalled". Zachariah is a variation of the name Zechariah. A biblical name; Zachariah was an Old Testament king of Israel.

Zachary

Pronunciation: ZAK-a-ree

The name Zachary is of Hebrew origin. The meaning of the name Zachary is "the Lord recalled". Zachary is a variation of the name Zachariah. A biblical name; Zachary is one of several names from the Old Testament.

Zach

Pronunciation: ZAK

The name Zack is diminutive of the several forms of Zachariah and Isaac.

Zahir

Pronunciation: ZA-hir

The name Zahir is of Arabic origin. The meaning of the name Zahir is "blossoming", "flourishing".

Zain

Pronunciation: zain

Zain is a variant of the Hebrew name Zane. It is also possibly a variant of the Hebrew name John. The meaning of the name Zain is "God is gracious".

Zander

Pronunciation: ZAN-der

Zander is of Greek and Slavic origin. The meaning of the name Zander is "man's defender". Zander is a short form of the name Alexander.

Zephaniah

Pronunciation: ze-pha-niah

The name Zephaniah is of Hebrew origin. The meaning of the name is "hidden by God". A biblical name; borne as a minor prophet.

Zeus

Pronunciation: ZOO-SE

Zeus is of Greek origin. The meaning of Zeus is "living". Zeus is the name of the chief of the Olympian gods, and father of the gods and goddesses.

Zion

Pronunciation: ZI-on

The name Zion is of Hebrew origin. The meaning of the name is "highest point". In the Christian religion, Zion is the name for heaven.

Banned baby names around the world

Although the UK and the USA have some of the most liberal rules in the world when it comes to baby names, other countries have created lists of banned names that you cannot name your child in their country.

The *Boy Baby Names for 2017* Book of Baby Names has put together some of the funniest and most bizarre banned baby names from around the world.

Mexico

The Mexican State of Sonora released a long list of names that are banned for reasons being that they are 'derogatory, pejorative, discriminatory or for simply lacking in meaning.' The list of prohibited names in Sonora include;

All Power	Petronilo
Batman	Pocahontas
Burger King	Privado
Cesárea	Rambo
Christmas Day	Robocop
Circuncisión	Rocky
Email	Rolling Stone
Espinacia	Terminator
Facebook	Sonora querida
Harry Potter	Telesforo
Hermione	Tránsito
Hitler	Twitter
Iluminada	Usnavy

James Bond	Virgen
Lady Di	Verulo
Masiosare	Yahoo
Micheline	Zoila Rosa

Saudi Arabia

Saudi Arabia released their list of banned baby names which include any names that have royal connotations such as prince or princess, names of prophets, western names are also included in the list. The list of forbidden baby names in Saudi Arabia include;

Abdul Naser	Loland
Al Mamlaka (The Kingdom)	Malaak (Angel)
Alice	Malika (Queen)
Amir (Prince)	Maline
Aram	Maya
Basmala (utterance of the name of God)	Nabi (Prophet)
Barrah	Nabiyya (Female Prophet)
Baseel	Nardeen
Bayan	Naris
Binyamin (Arabic for Benjamin)	Randa
Elaine	Rital
Iman	Rama (Hindu God)
Inar	Sandy

Jibreel (Angel Gabriel)	Sumuw (Highness)
Kibrial	Tabarak (Blessed)
Lareen	Tilaj
Lauren	Yara
Linda	Wireelam

Australia

Australian government has 'proposed names will not be registered if they are obscene or offensive, unreasonably long, contain symbols without phonetic significance or are not in the public interest for some other reason.' Some of the baby names banned in Australia include the following;

Batman	Maryjuana
Bonghead	Medicare
(Blankspace)	Ned Kelly
Chief Maximus	Osama
Circumcision	Panties
Chow Tow	Pieandsauce
Dick Head	Post Master General
G-Bang	President
Goose	#ROFL
Hitler	Ranga

Ice-T	Scrotum
Ikea	Shithead
iMac	Spinach
Jesus Christ	Smelly
Lol	Snort
Lucifer	Virgin
Martian	

Germany

German guidelines state that names must indicate the gender of the child and must not be likely to lead to humiliation. You are forbidden to use surnames or the names of objects or products as first names. In order to protect the child, the name must not be absurd or degrading in any way. Local registrars decide which names to approve and which ones to reject.

A Turkish couple who were living in Germany were refused the permission to call the child Osama Bin Laden. Gender Neutral names are also rejected such as the name Matti.

Amongst some of the banned baby names in Germany are;

Agfa	Osama Bin Laden
Atom Fired	Pillula
Gramopho	Puhbert
Bierstübl	Satan
Cain	Schnucki
Hitler	Schroeder

Judas	Sputnik
Lenin	Stompie
MC Donald	Troublemaker
Ogino	The number 'Pi'
Omo	Woodstock

China

In China, a couple tried to name their child Wang @. The symbol in Chinese is pronounced "ai-ta", which means "Love him." The parents claimed that the @ symbol echoed the love that they had for the child.

Malaysia

Malaysian authorities have also banned the use of numbers in baby names, Japanese car names and royal titles. A list of banned baby names has been published. Included on the list is the Canonese monikers Sor Chai which means Insane, Chow Tow, meaning Smelly Head. The use of Woti has also been discouraged as a baby name as it means sexual intercourse.

New Zealand

A court in New Zealand took over the guardianship of a young girl named, Talula Does The Hula From Hawaii so that they could change her name. The judge condemned the name and the rising trend of parents using wacky baby names, claiming that it would lead to bullying.

Another couple in New Zealand were banned from naming their twins Fish and Chips, although the name Number 16 Bus Shelter was approved by authorities.

Names on the list of banned baby names in New Zealand include;

Anal	Majesty
Baron	Major
Bishop	Messiah
Duke	President
Judge	Prince
King	Princess
Knight	Queen
Lady	Royale
Lucifer	

Portugal

Portugal has put a ban on parents using nicknames on their childs birth certificates. This means the name Tom would be rejected however the full name Thomas would be accepted.

Amongst the banned names in Portugal are;

Albuquerque
Ashanti
Ben-Hur
Brilhante
Britta Nórdica
Do Sorriso

Faruk
Mar E Sol (Portuguese for sean & sun)
Nazareth Fernades
Nirvana
Olaf
Portugal
Sandokan
Satélite
Sayonara (Japanese for goodbye)
Viking
Zingara (Italian for gypsy)

BIBLOGRAPHY

Cresswell, Julia
Bloomsbury Dictionary of First Names
Bloomsbury, London, 1992

Cross. F. L and Livingstone E A, ed
Oxford Dictionary of the Christian Church
Oxford University Press, 1997

Drunkling, Leslie
First names first
J M Dent & Sons Ltd, London 1977

Fergusson, Rosalind
Choose Your Baby's name
Penguin, London 1987

Hall, James
Dictionary of Subjects and Symbols in Art
John Murrary, 1992

Hanks, Patrick and Falvia Hodges
A Concise Dictionary of First Names
Oxford University Press, Oxford, 1997

Holy Bible
Cambridge University Press

Macleod, Iseabail and Terry Freedman
The Wordsworth Dictionary of First Names

Wordsworth Editions Limited, London, 1995

Office for National Statistics
Baby Names, England and Wales
Publish 2014

Pickering, David
The Penguin Dictionary of First Names
Penguin, 2004

Room, Adrian
Brewer's Names
Cassell, London, 1992

Stafford, Diane
The Big Book of 60, 000 Baby Names
Sourcebooks, Inc, 2006

Strong, James
Strong's Concordance of the Bible
Thomas Nelson 1980

Withycombe, E G
Oxford Dictionary of English Christian Names
Oxford University Press, Oxford 1977

Hannah Crawford

38006927R00093

Made in the USA
Middletown, DE
12 December 2016